CROSSING THE
POSTMODERN
DIVIDE

A L B E R T   B O R G M A N N

Crossing
the
Postmodern
Divide

THE UNIVERSITY OF   *Chicago and London*
CHICAGO PRESS

The University of Chicago Press, Chicago 60637
The University of Chicago Press, Ltd., London
© 1992 by The University of Chicago
All rights reserved. Published 1992
Paperback edition 1993
Printed in the United States of America
01 00 99 98 97 96 95 94   5 4

ISBN: 0-226-06626-6 (cloth)
ISBN: 0-226-06627-4 (paperback)

Library of Congress Cataloging-in-Publication Data

Borgmann, Albert.
     Crossing the postmodern divide / Albert Borgmann.
        p.   cm.
     Includes bibliographical references and index.
     1. United States—Civilization—1970—   .   2. Technology and
civilization.   3. Science and civilization.   I. Title.
E169.12.B666   1992
973.92—dc20   91-31971
                                                                        CIP

CONTENTS

ch. 0.

88949

ACKNOWLEDGMENTS

I am indebted to Daniel Kemmis for conversations on politics and community and to my colleagues from the Society for Philosophy and Technology, Carl Mitcham and Paul Durbin in particular, for long-standing support.

CROSSING THE
POSTMODERN
DIVIDE

1. CLOSURE AND TRANSITION

There is a rising sentiment that we are coming to the close not only of a century and a millennium but of an era, too. The sentiment has not quite become universal, yet the indications of closure and transition are manifold. One indication is the difficulty we have in finding the kind of discourse that would help us to chart the passage from the present to the future. The idiom we have favored since the beginning of the modern era fails to inspire conviction or yield insight; the language of those who are proclaiming a new epoch seems merely deconstructive or endlessly prefatory.

The distinctive discourse of modernity is one of prediction and control. In the teeth of severe cultural and moral crises, we continue to use it as if it were the sole alternative to sullen silence. Ironically, there is a profound helplessness in surrendering the future to prediction and control, and there would be even if we could predict and control things at will.

We predict the weather and try to control inflation because we are not the weather and not inflation. They are objects other than ourselves, objects we want to subject to ourselves. Strictly speaking, I do not predict or control myself or my behavior. I promise or decide to do a certain thing; I pledge myself to do it. I do not manipulate or arrange my behavior so that it proceeds to the desired outcome. I either do or fail to do what I set out to do.

Nor would I think of predicting and controlling others to whom I am bound by ties of respect and affection. It would not occur to me to assimilate them to the weather and inflation. Yet the dominant discourse about the future of our society is composed of the vocables of prognoses, projections, extrapolations, scenarios, models, programs, stimulations, and incentives. It is as though we had taken ourselves out of reality and had left only objectified and disavowed versions of ourselves in the universe we are trying to understand and shape. We vacate our first-person place and presence in the world just when we mean to take responsibility for its destiny. Surely there is deprivation and helplessness in this.

Liberals have been most determined collectively to plan and engineer society for the better. They, accordingly, have been associated most closely with the obstreperous problems of social policy and the vacancy of public discourse. To conservative minds, the sensible alternative to misguided liberal ambitions is a healthy respect for the natural order of things. We can affect the large design of society only in a negative manner. All we can do positively and collectively is step aside and allow the native ambitions of individuals and the spontaneous dynamics of small groups to take their beneficial course.[1]

But there is helplessness in this position, too, for it views social reality as a natural fact like the seasons and the weather, and urges us to make peace with it. Like liberals, conservatives feel bound to consider society objectively and prospectively, to determine the best future outcome given our present conditions. Here, too, the collective future is something that happens to people.

In bringing out the predictive and controlling intentions of modern discourse about the future, I am not concerned with highlighting the limits of social science or the seriousness of social and environmental problems. These are real enough. But even if we could overcome these obstacles, the crucial debility of the rule of prediction and control would remain, namely, the expatriate quality of public life. We live in self-imposed exile from communal conversation and action. The public square is naked. American politics has lost its soul. The republic has become procedural, and we have become unencumbered selves. Individualism has become cancerous. We live in an age of narcissism and pursue loneliness.[2] These expressions are alarming not because they predict the ruin of the state; prediction and control, for all their liabilities, will continue to provide comfort and stability. Rather, these expressions of distress should disquiet us because they indicate that we have no common life, that what holds us all together is a cold and impersonal design.

The language of postmodernism has crucial critical force. But

3

much of it seems idle; very little of it gives us a helpful view of the postmodern divide or of what lies beyond it. How can we hope, then, to find a discourse in which to explore this watershed and find our way across it? Much thought has been given to measures that might engender lively participation in an unconstrained conversation. Conditions have been laid down that need to be met if vital democracy is to be recovered. But for all their good intentions and careful erudition, these efforts are misguided and misleading.[3] The champions of good procedure post guards at the doors of city hall to prevent undemocratic types from entering. Inside, the tables and chairs have been arranged to achieve an order of equality and openness. But no one, in fact, enters, sits down, and begins to converse. The concern with the antecedent conditions of a participatory democracy or an ideal speech situation is an attempt at so controlling the common setting that genuinely democratic transactions and results can be predicted safely. But the preparatory efforts forever get in the way of what they try to make room for.

We have to venture out into the open, discover the landmarks and dwell on the particulars. We must share with each other what we have found instead of talking forever about manuals and compasses. Accordingly, I want to give an accounting and a recounting of how I see the postmodern divide rising from the plains of modernity and of the views that open up once we have left the modern realm behind. We might think of the rise of postmodernism as a vast and intricate mountain range. How can we hope to find our way through it? Certainly not by exploring it square foot by square foot. We must consider its major peaks and currents, and then choose some of them as landmarks for our journey. Every historical account has a particular point of departure, a particular goal in mind, and is guided by particular considerations, acknowledged or not.

While we are both required and free to select our landmarks, we are not at liberty to locate them at will. We must acknowledge their actual place and the ways they are related to each other. We ought to select those that are truly imposing and orienting. The landmarks I have chosen come in groups of three. That choice, I hope, will provide more memorable guidance than a less didactic schema would. Of course, landmarks taken in threes are unlikely to fall into a straight line. They describe, in fact, a path that winds back and forth between economy and culture, labor and leisure, science and technology, history and philosophy.

The schematic part of this essay gives us some distance on the expanse of the material and the mass of features we confront in exploring the end of the modern era. We need distance to comprehend and overcome modernity, but distance is not enough. To pass beyond the modern framework, we must allow things that are beyond the control of modernity to speak in their own right. Because narrative discourse is about things in particular, I will relate stories that others have told and recount things of my own observation.

Schematically speaking, this essay begins by noting the three features that distinguish the Middle Ages from the modern era: local boundedness, cosmic centeredness, and divine constitution. The events we associate with Columbus, Copernicus, and Luther shattered the medieval edifice and opened up vast areas of exploration and construction. For heuristic purposes, we can think of Bacon, Descartes, and Locke as the founders of a new era, the designers of the modern project whose elements are the domination of nature, the primacy of method, and the sovereignty of the individual. Technology and economy were the disciplines whereby the modern project was worked into a social order characterized by aggressive realism, methodical universalism, and an ambiguous individualism.

Toward the end of this century, realism, universalism, and individualism have become the subjects of withering critiques. Although the modern project still drifts ahead as a political and economic movement, it has lost its theoretical confidence and credibility. Yet the postmodern critique of modernism offers us no more than the weakest of constructive proposals: respect for nature, particularism, and communitarianism. One can detect a more concrete and consequential postmodern paradigm in the economy, a paradigm characterized by information processing, flexible specialization, and informed cooperation.

The postmodern condition is on the whole a striking departure from the modern project and a salutary response to the crisis of modernity. But it is still a deeply ambiguous constellation that may be resolved in two very different ways. One, which is the direct descendant of modern technology and is much more prominent at the surface of recent developments, I call hypermodernism. It is devoted to the design of a technologically sophisticated and glamorously unreal universe, distinguished by its hyperreality, hyperactivity, and hyperintelligence. Hypermodernism derives much of its energy from its supposed alternative, a sullen resignation to the decline of the modern era, a sullenness that is palpable, particularly in this country. There is, however, a way of life beyond sullenness and hyperactivity. It is a recovery of the world of eloquent things, a recovery that accepts the postmodern critique and realizes postmodern aspirations. I call this recovery postmodern realism and point up its emerging characteristics—focal realism, patient vigor, and communal celebration.

So much for the schematic aspect of this essay.[4] Of course, if my account were entirely schematic, it would not be an essay at all; it would be a treatise in the modern style. To get beyond the modern framework, we need an essay, an experiment, a venture. What force it has will lie in the particulars it recounts.

SULLENNESS   I begin with a tentative look at the national landscape. Describing a landscape is much like drawing a picture. In Henri-Georges Clouzot's film *The Mystery of Picasso* we are shown repeatedly the emergence of pictures and paintings.[5] There is always the first stroke, intriguing, commanding, and yet utterly indefinite. What does it foretell? How will it continue? As line is added to line, the initial ambiguity is resolved. A curve becomes a back, a body becomes a reclining figure, a woman reading a book, lying on a couch in front of a brightly patterned wall, and so forth. Our comprehension follows the gathering features until there is a complete picture. The procedure of rendering, however prosaically, the contemporary social vista is similar. It is a matter of drawing feature after feature of the nation's present mood. No one feature by itself is significant, but their configuration might well be.

The nation's mood is sullen. Although such sullenness is to be found in most advanced technological countries, it here takes on a peculiarly American visage. It displays various qualities and manifestations. Sullenness is both passive and aggressive, both indolent and resentful. It manifests itself both in obvious social maladies and in diffused and individual symptoms.

Indolence is often thought to be simply laziness. But as the etymology of the word suggests, indolent passivity is at bottom the incapacity to be pained by things undone and challenges unmet. One might think of this inability to respond as a sort of paralyzed irresponsibility. American indolence manifests itself in two obvious economic indicators. One is foreign debt. The United States is the foremost debtor nation in absolute terms. The trade imbalance reflects the difference between what people want to have and what they have actually earned. Americans are able to consume more than they are earning on the basis of what they have accomplished in the past. Now they are burning their furniture and pawning their heirlooms to keep warm.[6]

We find a milder version of this irresponsibility in the federal budget deficit. The deficit reflects the difference between the amount of government services people want and the amount they are willing to pay for through taxes. Without foreign indebtedness, this imbalance would be an internal matter—Americans borrowing from Americans to serve Americans. Foreign debt aside, a budget deficit bespeaks indolence anyway. It amounts to a purchase of present federal power and beneficence at the cost of less and less federal discretion in dealing with the nation's future challenges and maladies. As federal debt grows, an ever greater share of taxes goes to the creditors and with it the discretion that goes with money. Power shifts from public into private hands. The growth of federal indebtedness amounts to a spreading paralysis of government, a development one should have expected under Republican presidents.[7] At any rate, it represents a self-inflicted debilitation of this nation's integrity and vigor.

The popular will to self-discipline and self-government is flagging. This indolence appears not only in the irresponsible decisions of consumers and politicians but most fatally perhaps in the indifference of voters. In a democracy, the vote is the people's voice. It is the wellspring of political power and legitimacy. But in this country, it is a source of diminishing vigor. Since 1960, voter turnout has declined by 20 percent and is now the lowest of any democracy in the world.[8]

The common explanations of this trend amount to an exoneration of the people from the charge of indolence. There are chiefly two explanations: The first holds that the powerful and their functionaries have devised and protected a system of voter registration that discourages the poor and uneducated; the second alleges disenchantment and disgust with politics and blames television in particular for its negative and trivializing impact on politics. It must be conceded that voter registration *is* needlessly complicated in many places. Yet it is rarely more complicated than obtaining a driver's license or a television set, tasks that the vast majority of people have no trouble accomplishing.[9] It is also true that the poor and uneducated, potential supporters of the Democrats, are disproportionately numerous among nonvoters. But they are far from alone. In the 1988 presidential election, Republican participation declined by five percent while Democratic participation rose by nine tenths of one percent.[10] As for televised politics, people have not reacted by turning their sets off, nor have they overwhelmingly elected representatives committed to reform.

The majority of people who do vote exhibit the resentful side of sullenness. Sullenness becomes resentful when brooding displeasure and disability take on an aggressive and dismissive aspect. Resentment is sullen in that dissatisfaction does not lead to open and constructive action but rather turns to indirection and obstruction. Although these voters profess to support civil liberties and welfare measures, they finally resent effective measures to help the poor, the powerless, and those out of the cultural mainstream.[11] Their decisive concern and vote is for the vigor and advancement of prosperous inequality; their place in this arrangement is determined by envy for those above and reproach for those below.[12]

Some of the same people like to use moral issues, such as abortion and the death penalty, both to express and to disguise the disdain they have for their presumed inferiors. When members of the American middle and upper classes fervently support the correctness and severity of capital punishment, they are not holding themselves to a lofty moral norm, since no one of their kind is likely to be put to death. Rather, they condemn "a certain element" of the population— the poor racial minorities. Many people use a similar logic to withhold public funds for abortion. They do not oppose abortion across the board—in fact, they usually favor the right to abortion—but it is a right they prefer to exercise while punishing poor women for their supposed lack of caution and restraint.

A further social indicator of sullen resentment is the unemployment rate in this country. If we view it historically or internationally, it is not extraordinarily high, but it has been remarkably firm and uncontested. We have come to accept unemployment as the inevitable price of economic stability. If the demand for labor were raised above its usual level, wages would rise, inflation would ensue, and economic uncertainty would spread.

The depressing effects of unemployment in this country are disproportionately concentrated on one group, the blacks. Race is used to single out victims; once singled out, not only are they made to pay the price of stability, but they are also burdened with the responsibility for their own plight.[13] There is an alternate basis for economic stability, namely, the kind of solidarity that keeps wantonly rising wages in check. But this is just the kind of common discipline that resentment has been corroding.

Social resentment is prudent and constrained. It is concerned to protect the inequality that animates it. This resentful prudence is brought into relief through the way it is being tested by AIDS. The primary tendency of resentment is to confine this calamity to marginal groups. Such confinement makes the most straightforward and effective strategies of dealing with AIDS unavailable, that is, the voluntary, general, and mutually benevolent identification of infections; principled and organized support of victims; and the technically simple application of preventive measures. Having rejected that approach, the American mainstream generally bets on two hopes, the fonder one being for a technological fix providing a cure or prevention. Failing that, the other hope is that the disease will remain within socially demarcated and supposedly negligible groups.[14] If the second hope is disappointed also, measures to bring about a social confinement of the disease and to secure the traditional middle and upper class will be strengthened and multiplied.

A similar if less virulent problem is the widespread abuse of drugs. The most lethal drugs are alcohol and tobacco, which account for about four hundred thousand deaths annually. We have countered with halfhearted measures at best. At the same time, we have declared war on the illegal drugs that cause fewer than four thousand deaths each year, and we are spending about three billion dollars annually in waging that war.[15]

There are good reasons for vigorous concern about the drugs that have been declared illegal.[16] But our martial and self-righteous approach is but another expression of sullen resentment. We concentrate our fire on the drug-producing countries and on drug dealers.[17] We are becoming increasingly punitive with drug users, too, since, like AIDS, the use of heroin and cocaine does not pose a major threat to most middle-class Americans.[18] What we spare ourselves is a thoughtful and persistent consideration of the social conditions that favor the abuse of alcohol, tobacco, marijuana, cocaine, and heroin as well as a determination to help and heal the victims of drug abuse.

There are other social trends that bespeak sullenness: the decline of literacy, the lack of scientific understanding, the deplorable state of physical fitness, the cancerous growth of the video culture. But indolence and resentment show themselves not only in these broadly measurable phenomena but also in diffuse and anecdotal ways, in numberless incidents of careless service, shoddy work, wasted time, scattered trash, and mindless consumption. At times sullenness is voiced in telling phrases. Indolence comes to the fore in the expression, so often delivered with finality, "it's *my* choice." What sounds like the assumption of ultimate responsibility is usually the flourish of moral retreat, the refusal to discuss, explain, and justify a decision, and the retirement to self-indulgence.

When misery comes to our doorstep unexpected and uninvited, resentment rushes into the words: "I don't *need* that." What makes that expression so whiny and self-righteous? The words imply that someone mistakenly thought we *needed* a child, or a disabled parent, or a car wreck, or some other misfortune. And underlying that implication is the deeper assumption that one is the legitimate recipient only of things one incontestably needs. Since a burden is no such thing, it is incomprehensible at best and thought to be morally outrageous at worst.

The major encumbrance humans used to take on as a matter of course was children. Childlessness has become increasingly common in this as in all advanced technological societies. Traditionally, the burden of children fell heavily on women; so in part women more frequently remain childless in response to unjust and discommoding social arrangements. But there is also a more general resentment of parental obligation.[19]

To be sure, there are morally outrageous burdens, obstacles placed in our way by prejudice or oppression. Accordingly, the law has been well employed to remove or at least decrease racism and sexism. There also are burdens that ought to be shared because they can be. Workers who are injured or lose their jobs are entitled to relief through legally mandated insurance systems. But the common expectations of redress and compensation go much further. In fact, they go all the way: one expects to be compensated for any burden, no matter how it was incurred or suffered.[20] The legal system and the insurance industry have been extended and reshaped to serve as universal compensators and to produce something like total justice.

Total justice is the social accommodation to sullenness; it seems to be a peculiarly American response to indolence and resentment.[21] Take the doctrine of strict liability, which absolves one from having to use a jeep or a lawnmower with care and caution. This doctrine shifts the burden of any accident to the manufacturer, who is held strictly, that is, almost unconditionally, liable.[22] The doctrine acknowledges common indolence, people's inability to accept reasonable responsibility for their acquisitions and actions; it sanctions their resentment of pain and loss that follow from irresponsibility.[23]

Indolence exhibits a new shade of meaning when seen in the context of compensation for pain and suffering. Payments of this kind have a venerable history.[24] But the range of cases so compensable and the size of the payments have grown enormously of late, particularly in this country. Compensation now is allowed not only for physical pain resulting from an injury but also for mental anguish, and not only for mental anguish deriving from an injury but also from a traumatic experience, such as seeing a loved one die in an accident.[25]

Compensation for pain and suffering, of course, does not heal and make the person whole again. So what good does it do? Why should it be paid? One might say that since people spend money to avoid and prevent pain and suffering, they should receive money when misery is inflicted on them. Yet, while money keeps distress at bay in the former case, it fails to remove it in the latter. Might one argue, then, that compensation is the punishment a victim must be able to exact from the culprit? Apparently not, for victims do not as a rule feel resentment toward those who were the cause of their suffering.[26] Nor are large settlements sought from individuals and intended to pain them in return. The payments are exacted from insurance companies and ultimately provided by all policyholders. We must conclude that compensation is the public acceptance of indolence, understood as people's inability to find meaning in suffering, and the acceptance of resentment, resentment not of people but of inalienable pain.

On the surface, Americans are as optimistic as ever. In fact, there seems to have been a surge of optimism in the mid-eighties.[27] To observers from abroad, this appears to be a self-centered and precarious show of confidence, a disengagement from the realities of the globe, perhaps not too different, at bottom, from the sullenness that is most evident in the widespread and sometimes angry disavowal of responsibility.[28]

These concluding considerations of sullenness provide a hint of the deeper issue that lies beneath indolence and resentment. Reality in a strong and focal sense is what comes to us in its own right, as unforethinkable joy and as inescapable pain. I want to suggest that we are in danger of losing our sense of reality. Even if one applauds the attempt to salve unavoidable suffering with money, one should wonder whether the attitude that begets such attempts will not also rob us of real joy.

HYPERACTIVITY   Not all the features of sullenness are equally prominent. Those reflected in the obvious decline of this country's global position are the most evident, since a nation's rank in the world is determined by its economic power. Hence, economists often are thought to have the clearest view of the nation's morose condition and the most effective prescription for a cure.

Given the complexity of physician and patient, the economic diagnosis and therapy of national sullenness are astoundingly clear and uncontested. The physician, in this case, is the economic profession, a social science afflicted with softness and a dearth of powerful explanatory laws; the patient is our pluralistic and diverse society. The symptoms of our malady are the slowing growth of our standard of living and our declining strength in international competition. To combat the underlying causes, we must increase taxes, savings, expenditures for capital equipment, for research and technology, for the infrastructure, and for the improvement of the labor force; we must decrease government spending and consumption; and, finally, we must strengthen the coordination of the public and private sectors.[29]

In addition to having wide assent, this view of our situation is remarkable for the way it conceals the kind of effort needed to bring about reform. The economic measures we need to raise our standard of living and restore our economic power have been spelled out and justified with clinical precision; accordingly it appears that all we need to do is restore and fire up the economic machinery of this country. This task, of course, requires a measure of attention and discipline, but essentially it appears to be nothing more than reasonable and prudent. In truth, however, the standard cure is a prescription for hyperactivity. To be sure, some of the proposed therapeutic measures are sound and conducive to thrift, but taken together and subordinated to the standard goals, they will transform us into a hyperactive society.

"Hyperactive" is a respectable nineteenth-century word, first recorded in 1867.[30] A century later the term emerged as a label for unruly youngsters whose inattentive and impatient energy led educators to suspect a definite illness. Although they could tell a hyperactive child when they saw one, not until recently have researchers been able to find a definite underlying cause that would hold up to scrutiny.[31]

I want to use "hyperactive" in the wider cultural sense that is roughly present in the shortened adjective "hyper." There are close analogies between the clinical and cultural versions of the syndrome. To the distracted energy of the clinical case there corresponds a nervous restlessness in the cultural type. Where the patient suffers from a greatly shortened attention span, the cultural counterpart exhibits an extremely narrowed focus on the world and its variety. And finally, while clinically hyperactive people seem intractable, culturally hyperactive persons appear intolerant of their more placid humans. There is also a radical disanalogy. The clinical syndrome is commonly judged alarming and in need of therapy; the cultural version is revered and recommended as the cure for the nation's ills.

What will a truly hyperactive society be like? One way of capturing its character is to think of it as a state of mobilization where the richness and variety of social and cultural pursuits and the natural pace of daily life have been suspended to serve a higher, urgent cause. Today's leaders show instances of such mobilization. They work long and arduous hours; family, culture, and religion are unconditionally subordinated to the pursuit of success. The stress of long tours of duty is briefly interrupted by episodes of exotic rest and recreation. Of course, even under conditions of general, if not total, mobilization, few will struggle at the forefront of progress. But all others are on notice that their relative peace is undeserved and insecure, and that at any moment they may be evacuated, conscripted, or discharged. More precisely, we can say that the mobilized and hyperactive society exhibits three features that need to be examined: the suspension of civility, the rule of the vanguard, and the subordination of civilians.

The suspension of civility is no trivial matter; it presupposes a fervent dedication to the goals on whose behalf civil and genteel pursuits are curtailed. The mobilization must verge on a jihad. I am not sure the goals of a rising standard of living and global economic leadership will call forth such fervor in this country. I would be distressed if they did. In any case, we ought to realize that extreme devotion is in fact implied in the standard proposals for economic action.

Assuming, then, intense and widespread dedication to the twin economic goals, the claims of civility will be suspended. We can already see the beginnings of such measures both in the social realm and in personal circumstances. By the claims of civility I mean humanitarian and cultural programs, which have suffered in our attempts to reduce the federal deficit. Legal aid, public aid for housing construction, enforcement of civil rights, and health and safety regulations in the workplace have been cut back. Support for basic research, for the arts and humanities has been weakened.

What argues for the suspension of civility also explains the necessity of a vanguard. The proximate origin of compulsion is international competition. Increasingly since World War II, it has become more single-minded and radical. Traditional constraints of comfort, comity, and territory have been dissolved by a reckless curiosity and dedication. To excel internationally in any discipline now requires, with the exception of a few preternaturally lucky or gifted stars, the risk of one's capacities under extreme pressure.

This development springs primordially from the recession of reality that will occupy us more directly later. Let me simply suggest here that the richness and subtlety of nature, art, and religion have been fading before our eyes. Or perhaps we have become impatient with difficulty and depth of meaning and therefore have insisted that complexity and ambiguity be reduced and hardened into unequivocal measures and magnitudes. This is suggested by political elections where what should be an occasion for reflection and affirmation has been narrowed to the military enterprise of a campaign. The campaign has been conceived more narrowly still as a race where the candidates' positions are incessantly ascertained by polls. Debates, which are not likely to be rich in subtlety or complexity anyhow, have no real meaning for us until they have been given a score through the polls.

To compensate for the one-dimensional and trite character of score-keeping, competitors of all kinds are expected to risk their very substance. They are often eager to do so because the invigoration of life through the devotion to a precise, demanding, and widely admired task is felt even more intensely by the actor than the spectator. A life devoted to such competition has awesome simplicity, splendor, and fragility; its goal is perfectly well-defined, its success universally applauded, and its welfare ever imperiled.

Let Boyd L. Jefferies stand as an example.[32] In 1962 he cofounded the brokerage firm that bears his name. His success was evident in the growth of his firm, the size of the takeovers he helped to forge, and the salary he commanded. He prospered by breaking down the traditional limits of business, particularly the limit of a day's work. His firm was at work at all hours, night and day. And so, very nearly, was he. He would rise at 1:30 or 2:30 A.M., drive to work, and often stay until 7:00 P.M.

He loved his work; he was obsessed and intoxicated with it. He would do anything to make his business grow. But life and work were perilous, too. "Had I stayed in business," he has said, "I probably would have worked myself to death." It did not come to that because, while shattering traditional barriers of business, Mr. Jefferies also overstepped the boundaries of the law. Once indicted, he made an agreement with prosecutors to serve as a witness. Thereupon he was released from the vise of his narrow and pressing obsession. His life became calmer and more varied: he divided his time between homes in California and Colorado; he dabbled in venture capital enterprises and during the summers ran a golf clinic for children; he spent time with his three grandchildren. And yet "he's a man lost without his profession," his lawyer said. Mr. Jefferies fervently believed "there's a bright star in my future." That star was the business he hoped to return to.

Such hyperactive work habits can be found among most members of this country's power elite, among the leading lawyers, politicians, bureaucrats, journalists, scientists, physicians, and scholars.[33] There is religious fervor in this devotion to hyperactivity. It provides direction in the face of idleness and doubt and serves as the warrant of individual accomplishment and collective salvation. Parents commend it to their children. It is what we know each of us should be dedicated to if only we were strong enough.

Most of us are not strong enough, however. Hyperactivity is the burden and privilege of the vanguard at the forefront of economic and technological progress. Yet the civilians on the home front live under the sway of hyperactivity, too. They work shorter hours under less pressure, yet these circumstances are anything but marks of leisure and sovereignty. Rather, they bespeak the idleness and dependence of the civilians who owe their good fortune to the exertion of the shock troops and in return must follow the commands of the vanguard and make whatever sacrifices the struggle for economic supremacy demands.

The weakness of civilians is apparent in the disposability of the noncombatant work force. The vanguard disposes of workers in a number of ways. It is free to determine the size of the work force according to the requirements of economic productivity and stability. If relatively few or fewer can be conscripted profitably, so many more will remain unemployed. The vanguard can adjust wages downward if international competition requires it, and, above all, the fighting elite is entitled to employ and dismiss the supporting troops as opportunity or difficulty dictate it. In more explicit economic terms, the subordination of civilians shows itself in the rise of the Japanese style of management, in the high level of unemployment, in the stagnation of real full-time wages, and in the growth of contingent labor. The first and last of these phenomena are the most revealing.

Japanese management also goes by the name of the "team concept" and recently has been called "management by stress."[34] These diverging appellations indicate that in Japanese management workers are brought into close proximity to hyperactivity, yet they remain excluded from the status and powers of the vanguard. According to the team concept, workers are divided into groups, responsibility for a portion of the production process is given to the group as a whole, and the cooperation of the group in making production more efficient is solicited and honored.

All this makes for more integrated and affirmative conditions of production and yields massive gains in productivity. At the same time, the system, because of its tighter structure, is more susceptible to pressure and more open to inspection. Pressure is typically exerted through speeding up the production process; the limits of the system show up in breakdowns. This is management by stress. Since there is no slack in the system, problems cannot be concealed. Beyond a certain point, the workers do not want to hide them. They know that their suggestions for repairing the weak points of the system will be heard.

Of course, there is a thin line between stress as a diagnostic tool and stress as a goad to more strenuous exertion. The workers have no part in drawing that line, nor in drawing up the larger design within which they work. They have become mere allies, perhaps accomplices, of hyperactivity. But they remain barred from hyperactive sovereignty, from the glory of battling in the front ranks of the struggle for global hegemony. Not surprisingly, the champions of the workers are divided: some deplore the hard and pressing conditions that ultimately confine the workers; others defend the legitimacy and utility of the agreement the workers have entered into.

The other phenomenon that reveals the subordination of the

commoners is the growth of the contingent work force.[35] The latter consists of all the workers who do not have secure or full-time work and the social provisions that normally go with it, such as protection against arbitrary dismissal, insurance and retirement benefits, and paid vacation. Some workers like the flexibility of part-time or temporary work. Most, however, prefer the stability of steady work, a foreseeable career, and social welfare. But the economic arrangement that the workers value as a sturdy and hospitable edifice is a slow and cumbersome behemoth to hyperactive ambition. In the strenuous and volatile conditions of international competition, an opportunity must be quickly exploited, a setback must be met resiliently, and labor resources must be shifted and deployed quickly. To the degree that this vision of a mobilized economy gains popular acceptance, common tolerance for the dismantling of social welfare in the realm of labor will grow. The uncertainty and hardships of the poorly employed are the sacrifices that must be made in the rear if the battle at the forefront of the global economy is to be won.

As in a country mobilized for war, the break between the vanguard and the civilians in a fully hyperactive society would not be abrupt. Some would clearly battle in the first rank while others would tarry in relative calm. In between, however, there are many degrees of involvement. In this country, the division between the forefront and home front is even less distinct as we are mainly caught in sullenness, even if we are often admonished to bestir ourselves into hyperactivity.

How real is the prospect of full-blown hyperactivity? It is certainly a technically feasible and psychologically sustainable social order. Japan is the ever-extolled example of a hyperactive society. It has launched itself into frenetic productivity, or perhaps simply resumed it after its defeat in the Second World War, and has sustained its efforts to universal admiration and envy. Great Britain, appearing on its way toward an egalitarian and civilized society after the war, lapsed into resentful and indolent economic disaster in the seventies. At the close of the decade, Margaret Thatcher sounded the fanfare of a hyperactive revolution and for more than a decade enjoyed a mandate to rouse Britain to economic competition and progress. She, too, has earned the admiration of the world community.

But in both of these cases, thoughtful observers have seen the dark side of hyperactivity. Robert Bellah has said that "Japan is a mobilized society, administered from the top down."[36] And Ronald Dworkin has remarked that those "who loved Britain for its community and political culture in the 1960's . . . will love it less now."[37] It seems that the pursuit of the ever-outstanding goal of global economic leadership dislodges societies from tradition and civility, from their place and pleasure here and now. All aspirations and endeavors are directed elsewhere, that is, toward the global economy and the coming economic results. Nations become expatriated in their own country. This dislocation began with the modern era. If we are to avoid its ultimate conclusion, we must attend to its initial condition.

2. MODERNISM

THE RISE OF
MODERNISM

The feeling that the modern period is coming to its end and that we are entering the postmodern era is not new. A generation ago, the flurry of observations about epochal changes in the social and cultural landscape precipitated a shower of "post-" terms—postcapitalist, postideological, postindustrial, and others.[1] Daniel Bell's 1973 book *The Coming of Post-Industrial Society* was a monument to these arguments. But, as Bell notes, in 1917 Arthur J. Penty already foresaw, or at any rate, fervently wished for, the postindustrial state.[2] The millennial sentiment has been rising again, gaining momentum through its breadth and variety. "Postmodern" is now the vocable favored to invoke a sense of closure and transition. Whatever its faults, the term reminds us of what needs to be understood before it can be overcome, namely, the modern period, its character and its boundaries.

To discern the final contours of modernity, it will be helpful to look back at the way the period and its name emerged. "Modern" comes from the Latin word *modo*, meaning "just now." It originally meant something like recent, present, or contemporary. The desire to distinguish one's culture from its predecessors arose as soon as something like a historical consciousness of culture had dawned in classical antiquity. Already in the first half of the second century B.C.E., the Greek grammarian Aristarchus distinguished the "newer" poets from the ancient Homer. Some such predecessor of "modern" was used henceforth until, in the late fifth century C.E., Latin begot the very word and bequeathed it to the emerging Middle Ages.[3] Evidently, the medieval period, both as a designation and as a historically bounded epoch, arose together with the awareness that a new era was dawning.[4]

The lesson we can draw from these terminological considerations is that historical periods in the West have issued from a rising sentiment of disaffinity, from a growing feeling that the kinship with what had gone before was being attenuated and lost. The break with the past was voiced in the most formal and general way: that was then, this is now; those were the ancients, we are the moderns.[5] This phenomenon appears to repeat itself in the generality of the term "postmodern." If history is to be trusted, "postmodernism" rather than a substantive term like "the information age" will be the name of the coming era.

Though the epoch-making sentiments are historically voiced in this broad and nearly vacuous manner, they do respond to profound and substantive events. When one considers the numerous and varied markers that have been staked at either boundary of the Middle Ages, one is easily persuaded that the bounding of epochs is not a mechanical or cogent enterprise.[6] Rather, it bespeaks a common conversation that, in our case, must respond to the real powers of nature and culture that modernism eclipsed.

Modernism now has become global, but it arose from the intensely local circumstances of the medieval epoch. Medieval culture began in halting and uncertain ways; it achieved its definition and grandeur as an accomplishment whereas modernism has always been a program or a project. The medieval epoch was clearly at hand when, at the turn of the ninth century, Charlemagne succeeded in fusing three disparate elements: the culture and learning of classical antiquity, the feudal order of the Germanic tradition, and, most important, the spiritual vision of Christian religion.

The achievement of the Middle Ages rests like a shadow of reproach on modernity, never more so than in the latter's late and closing years. Chivalry and courtesy, community and celebration, authority and craft are the residual forms of medieval excellence that are being dissolved before our eyes. But the vigor of the medieval order was spent by the late fifteenth century. Unlike the slow and convulsive decay of Greek and Roman culture, the medieval form of life came to a swift and unambiguous end. It was shattered by the three blows that we commonly associate with Columbus, Copernicus, and Luther.

All three of these men lived at the turn from the fifteenth to the sixteenth century. As we can see in retrospect, in discovering new worlds they jointly shattered the edifice of the old and opened up vast new areas of exploration and invention. The medieval world was, like all premodern cultures, a locally bounded, cosmically centered, and divinely constituted world. The Columbian discovery of the New World ruptured the familiar and surveyable geography of the Middle Ages. The Copernican solar system decentered the earth from its privileged position in the universe. The Lutheran reformation, in making the Bible and the believer the final authorities of Christianity, fatally weakened the communal power of divinity.[7] This is to put things schematically, looking back from a postmodern standpoint. And yet the force of these changes was felt fully by John Donne within a short century when he said:

> The Sunne is lost, and th'earth, and no mans wit
> Can well direct him, where to looke for it.
> And freely men confesse, that this world's spent,
> When in the Planets, and the Firmament
> They seeke so many new; they see that this
> Is crumbled out againe to his Atomis.
> 'Tis all in pieces, all cohaerence gone;
> All just supply, and all Relation:
> Prince, Subject, Father, Sonne, are things forgot,
> For euery man alone thinkes he hath got
> To be a Phoenix, and that there can bee
> None of that kinde, of which he is, but hee.[8]

Continuing the story of modernity's birth, we must note that, again unlike the fallen empire of Rome, the shattered Middle Ages did not lie in ruins for long. Less than a generation separates the last of the destroyers of the medieval order from the first of the founders of modernity, Francis Bacon. Bacon, along with René Descartes and John Locke, laid the theoretical foundations for the project I will call modernism (using "modernity" to designate the modern era).[9] We can speak more specifically still of the three foundational documents of modernism: Bacon's *New Atlantis* (1627), Descartes's *Discourse on Method* (1637), and Locke's *Second Treatise of Civil Government* (1690).[10]

All three treatises are pleas as much as proclamations. They plead for a new order and derive much energy from their indictment of medieval disorder, the duress of daily life, the deadwood of tradition, and the oppression of hierarchy and community. They urge a new fundamental agreement, one that razes the tottering and constricting medieval structures and begins anew on a solid fundament.

Bacon's dissatisfaction was focused on the unprincipled and disorganized state of scientific inquiry. His impatience was fueled by a new understanding of the hardness of human life. Although he saw human weakness in the face of nature as a consequence of the Fall, this religious orientation had lost its real force. It showed how our misery began, but it no longer indicated how we were to come to terms with it. For the visionary women of the Middle Ages, illness was a trial, a call to a new life, a being possessed by divinity, the experience of mystical death, or the wrestling with the burden of writing.[11] Bacon used religion to cover his flanks in his quest for human betterment.[12] But essentially human misery was for him, as it has remained for us, a needless and insufferable scandal that was to be overcome through the domination of nature.

Bacon not only taught modernity to stand up to the ancient scourges of humanity; he also identified the New World discovered by Columbus as an adversary that had to be brought to its knees. The conquest of the New World, of course, was not literally the execution of Bacon's project. Historical developments rise like freshets. While theorists are minor sources of such currents, they serve as major indicators of the way things are moving. At any rate, Bacon's violent language of torturing, extorting, and subjugating nature for human benefit sharply outlines for us, as it must have for many of his contemporaries, the modern approach to reality, to the burdens of daily life, and to the expanses of wild nature.[13]

The *New Atlantis* is celebrated as a program of modern research and technology, although little more than a quarter of the text is devoted to the schematic sketch of the research and development enterprise in Bacon's utopia. Most of the story is intended to dislodge readers from their medieval acquiescence to the traditions and miseries of their time, to persuade them that the domination of nature was urgent and beneficial. Bacon recognized the need for a radically new start, and he was ever eager to fill in the details of the new design. But he had little to say on method in the *New Atlantis* and rather reveled in picturing the research facilities of Salomon's House, the model of all scientific and technological institutes to come.

Descartes, to the contrary, argued that the radicality of procedure was crucial. The project of radical reconstruction, he held, would live or die by two requirements: first was the discovery of an absolutely unshakable foundation, to be attained by the fearless clearing away of all existing institutions; second was a constructive method of irresistible cogency. Once these requirements were met, all particular problems could be solved readily. More important, the Cartesian program provided a solution to the Copernican problem of how to cope with a disoriented world, one that no longer had a dominant center and privileged dimensions. Method promises order without recourse to orientation.

This is the triumph of procedure over substance. Bacon was still fascinated with the substantive features and details of the New World. In the *Discourse*, Descartes used concrete illustrations merely to demonstrate the power of his procedure. The thrust of the very first part of his treatise is to urge that without a powerful procedure, substantive accomplishments would be forever dubious and deficient; given a cogent procedure, however, any substantive result could be obtained easily and assuredly.

Like Bacon, Descartes appears to have made religion the pivot of his method. But rationality is the true warrant; God and theology are immaterial decorations, mere concessions to tradition. Descartes further excepted the social and political orders from radical reconstruction. This, too, was a compromise with the exigencies of his time. But the implication is obvious that the monarchical and traditional order was in need of reform.

Half a century later, Locke drew up a design that spelled out the social implications of the modern project. As Bacon was searching for the "proper foundations" and Descartes was determined to "start again from the very beginning," so Locke was concerned with recasting political power by deriving it from its "original," that is, from its fundamental condition.[14] This he found in the state of nature, governed by reason, which in turn derived from God. Once more the modern project seems to be suspended from divine authority. But the reformation movements, beginning with Luther, had shaken and shattered the communal authority of religion. What looks like a religious mooring in Locke's *Treatise* is but a traditional embellishment.

There is an element of disguise in the state of nature and the rule of reason, too. These notions lead us to expect an encompassing and stately common order. In fact, however, Locke's *Treatise* is a celebration of the individual, the unencumbered and autonomous human being.[15] Nature and reason are little more than indistinct backdrops for the individual. The autonomy of the single self is the new authority of last appeal. The common order arises from individuals through an agreement, and this contract remains subservient to the individual.

We can think of modernism as the conjunction of Bacon's, Descartes's, and Locke's projects, as the fusion of the domination of nature with the primacy of method and the sovereignty of the individual. Again, the story so told is schematic and pointed, but it has exerted its power on the culture at large. The triumvirate portrayed here had a close and powerful variant in Thomas Jefferson's life. Writing to John Trumbull from Paris in 1789, regarding the acquisition of busts and pictures, he says:

> I will put off till my return from America all of them except Bacon, Locke and Newton, whose pictures I will trouble you to have copied for me: and as I consider them as the three greatest men that have ever lived, without any exception, and as having laid the foundation of those superstructures which have been raised in the physical and moral sciences, I would wish to form them into a knot on the same canvas, that they may not be confounded at all with the herd of other great men.[16]

Jefferson's perception of the modern project endures to this day. He saw it as a cultural enterprise or, more precisely, as having its proper place and force in the realms of knowledge and conduct. This way of looking at modernism asserts itself in the term we commonly use for the modern project—Enlightenment. We think of the Enlightenment as the liberating dawn of reason that dispelled the darkness of medieval superstition and dogmatism, oppression and authoritarianism. We have deeply internalized the enlightened vision of reality. What Jefferson called the superstructures of the physical and moral sciences have been realized in the institutions of science and democracy. In the Western world, democracy and the commitment to equality are now so much a part of everyone's mental constitution that it would be comical to suspect anyone of being a closet monarchist. It would be rare to find a frank attempt at securing feudal distinctions through legislation. Similarly, the acceptance of the scientific worldview is in all serious regards unchallenged.

Of course, the progress of the Enlightenment project has not been smooth or steady. There was reason to despair of it in Hitler's Germany and Stalin's Russia. Nor is the revolution of the Enlightenment completed. This is consistent with the character of the modern project. Modernism began as a program and has remained one. It has continued to search out and destroy traditional structures and constrictions; it has been most confident in devising powerful procedures and machineries to fill the newly empty spaces. But with *what* does it fill them? The answer to this question has been forestalled by the expatriate fixation of modernism on a distant time and another place, the modernist alibi.

One must have numerous reservations about this modern lack of center and closure. None can be more distressing, however, than our failure to complete the social plank in the Enlightenment platform.[17] There is harsh and stubborn inequality in this country and among nations. There are reversions to superstition and prejudice. To avoid all misunderstanding, let me state my wholehearted commitment to the completion of the Enlightenment revolution in its social and scientific aspects, to fair equality of opportunity for women, blacks, Native Americans, homosexuals, and minorities generally, and to the promotion of pure scientific research and the acceptance of its well-confirmed results.

Still, it is evident that the social movement of the Enlightenment project has stalled. People no longer rally around the flag of equal liberty. Hence it is a mistake to press on with the Enlightenment program to the exclusion of all other inquiries and directions. The old Enlightenment guard has lost its audience and is effectively failing its obligation to equality. Unless we consider why the campaign for equality has run into a thicket of indifference and invidiousness, there is no hope for reinvigoration.

The challenge of this question is not one of precision but of width and depth. It is naive simply to insist on social justice as the criterion by which to judge the modern project rather than to recognize it as a strand that is deeply enmeshed in the fabric of modernism. We therefore must come to understand, through schemes and stories, how the domination of nature, the primacy of method, and the sovereignty of the individual were complicated into the modern project and how that project in turn rendered justice a complex and complicitous phenomenon.

AGGRESSIVE   The modern domination of nature was not
REALISM   an aristocratic assumption of the reins of
power but a violent campaign of conquest. It began with the voyages of discovery at the beginning of the modern period, with the expansion of trade routes, with extensive harnessing of wind and water power, with the establishment of manufactures for mass consumption, with the development of bookkeeping methods and financial instruments. Expansion within these limits soon ran up against insuperable barriers. Water flows and waterways, confined to certain locations, are subject to freezing, floods, and droughts. Wind power is limited to certain times. The strength, speed, and endurance of horses take a traveler only so far. How far? In 1830, a day's travel from New York took you to the easternmost parts of a few New England states. A week's travel opened the eastern seaboard up to Appalachia. It took six weeks to reach Lake Michigan.[18] And there were limits not only to the moving and shaping of things but also to the materials from which they were made. Stone is brittle and heavy; timber grows slowly; metals were hard to come by.

All of these barriers were shattered by coal, steam, and iron in the late eighteenth century and by dynamite in the middle of the nineteenth.[19] A particularly striking illustration of the explosive force of these developments is the expansion of the railroad system across the North American continent. The first railroad appeared in the United States in 1830. By 1850, New England and the South had something like a railroad network; by 1860, rails had reached the Midwest. On May 10, 1869, crews working from east and west joined their tracks into a transcontinental line at Promontory Point, Utah. By the turn of the century, the country was covered with nearly 200,000 miles of track. The peak of about 250,000 was reached in 1920. Today the mileage has fallen to where it was roughly a century ago.[20]

The conquest of the open American West was particularly dramatic. In Europe, a new transportation system was inserted into an old environment, one that was removed from the pristine state of nature and the original human condition of tribal hunting and gathering by thousands of years. This intrusion was painful enough. When a railroad was planned through England's Lake District in 1844, Wordsworth wrote a sonnet in protest and had it published in the *Morning Post* of October 16.

> *On the Projected Kendal and Windermere Railway*
> Is then no nook of English ground secure
> From rash assault? Schemes of retirement sown
> In youth, and 'mid the busy world kept pure
> As when their earliest flowers of hope were blown,
> Must perish;—how can they this blight endure?
> And must he too the ruthless change bemoan
> Who scorns a false utilitarian lure
> 'Mid his paternal fields at random thrown?
> Baffle the threat, bright Scene, from Orrest-head
> Given to the pausing traveller's rapturous glance:
> Plead for thy peace, thou beautiful romance
> Of nature; and, if human hearts be dead,
> Speak, passing winds; ye torrents, with your strong
> And constant voice, protest against the wrong.[21]

Forty years later, the surveyor Edward Gilette was locating a line for the Burlington Railroad through Nebraska territory. Only Native Americans and cowboys had preceded him in this wild and open country. "The cowboys were amazed to see a railroad party," Gilette wrote in his memoirs. "No one could believe that a railroad would penetrate that wild region."[22] Gilette and his crew had to carry their supplies into the snowy wastes of the winter of 1885, always in danger of losing orientation and life in the forbidding vastness of Nebraska's sand hills.

The surveyor was followed by the right-of-way agent who bought the land from farmers and ranchers. Often, however, the right-of-way crossed huge stretches of unclaimed and unsettled land. In such cases, the government gave a railroad company, on delivery of its promise to build a line, the right-of-way and hundreds of square miles of adjacent or additional land. But the land was not really there for the taking by the U.S. government or anyone else. The Native Americans had been here for thousands of years.

In late August and early September 1882, Assistant Attorney General Joseph Kay McCammon met with Arlee, Adolphe, Eneas, and Michelle, the chiefs of the Flatheads, Pend d'Oreilles, and Kootenais of the Flathead Reservation in northwestern Montana. McCammon had been appointed by the Secretary of the Interior to negotiate a right-of-way agreement for the transcontinental line of the Northern Pacific Railroad to run through the reservation.

These Native Americans had been moved repeatedly from their ancestral lands in Idaho and Western Montana, and were eventually confined to the Flathead Reservation. They wanted to be left alone on the last remnant of their country. "I want to remain in my country quiet and undisturbed," said Arlee.[23] But once more he was being pressed by the modern conquest of the continent. It was represented by a federal official representing a private corporation; and behind the corporation was a rising flood of miners, loggers, dam builders, farmers, and merchants.

Condescension and accommodation were mingled in the way McCammon personified all these forces in the Great Father. "I have been sent," he said, "by the Great Father at Washington a great many miles to see you and talk with you." When the chiefs demurred, he warned:

> The Great Father will be sorry when he hears that the Indians do not believe in his good faith. Shall I go back and say to the Great Father that these Indians do not believe he is treating them right? He has but one object, and that is your good; and if I go back without your having named a price for the lands, he will say they are not the good Indians and faithful friends I thought.[24]

The Native Americans in reply appealed to the terms of the treaty that had established the reservation. They proposed an alternative route, one that, in fact, was taken by later railroad lines. They reminded McCammon of the disruptions the railroad would inflict on their lives. They asked for what the strip of land was worth to them, a million dollars. They invoked the Native American understanding of the land. "My country was like a flower," Eneas said at one point, "and I gave you its best part." Arlee said, "You seem to like your money, and we like our country; it is like our parents."[25]

It was all in vain. McCammon spoke with the veiled impatience of a man who was unshakable in his convictions and certain of his power. Eventually the chiefs were reduced to asking for a thousand dollars more than they had been offered at first and to asking for cash rather than annuities. They were granted the first request; the second would be granted, so they were told, at the discretion of the Great Father.

Had the railroad run alongside the Clark Fork River from Missoula to its confluence with the Flathead River as Chief Eneas had requested, the Northern Pacific would have been burdened with another thirty miles of track.[26] Below this point, however, there was no escaping from burdens as the line followed the Clark Fork on its way to Idaho through a narrow canyon whose conquest required massive and brutal force. "Here and there in the cañon," a contemporary account says, "elevated benches of a few miles in length occur, which were eagerly occupied by the engineers as welcome respites to the enormous labor of digging and blasting a roadbed out of rocky walls or precipitous and treacherous slopes; but a considerable part of the line is steep side-hill work of blasting through places where the mountains thrust bare shoulders of rock into the river."[27]

To clear a grade in the canyon wall, the use of dynamite at first imitated the way of the human hand, cutting the rock from the top little by little until a bench had been opened up. J. L. Hallett, the chief engineer, devised a new method: He pushed numerous T-shaped tunnels below the intended grade into the side of the mountain and set them off all at once. "The effect was stupendous," says the chronicler, "the whole side of the mountain wall being lifted up and hurled into the river." Cuts through the mountain were similarly excavated. "One cut 24 feet deep by 400 feet long was excavated by a single blast of giant powder." Nature stood in the way of the line's progress not only through lapidary resistance but through destructive movement, too. "In April, 1883," we are told, "a surface area of forty acres, covered with trees, slid off into the river. The track sunk down to a depth of sixty feet below the grade, and a chasm was opened 1,300 feet in length."[28]

Impatience made the enterprise run into more obstacles. Construction was pushed ahead through the winter snow. "Thousands of men were engaged at times in shoveling the snow from the line in order that the grading and track-laying might proceed."[29] Massive amounts of dynamite and massive numbers of people were used to construct the railroads. Hallett had nine hundred Chinese and eight hundred white men working under him.[30] Many of them, "fresh from the steerage of immigrant ships," were used for construction and discarded when no longer needed.[31]

Prostitution, drinking, gambling, and violence accompanied the construction crews. James H. Kyner was a railroad contractor who graded lines for the Union Pacific in Nebraska and southern Idaho. To establish his authority among the workers, he occasionally had to assault them physically and prove himself adept with a gun. To pay his men their wages, he had to dodge the highwaymen, racing on a buckboard through the dead of night from the bank to the construction camp.[32] "Gentleness and consideration were almost unknown," Kyner says in his autobiography. "Thick skins, brute force, and constant determination were almost essential, and they were common enough attributes around our camps in those days."[33]

On occasion, the harshness of the campaign to dominate nature comes sharply into view. Though the route through the Flathead Reservation spared the Northern Pacific distance and difficulties, it did require the spanning of two deep gulches near Missoula. The larger gulch called for a trestle 226 feet high and 860 feet long. The trestle, first constructed of wood, was replaced by a steel structure in the winter of 1885.[34] Charles Healy of Chicago was in charge of the work. His wife accompanied him, gaining everyone's admiration when she fearlessly walked across the timbers of the bridge, carrying her baby with her. One morning Healy stepped off a flatcar on the bridge, slipped, and fell to his death. He was taken to a nearby saloon and laid on the billiard table. When Mrs. Healy was called, "all she could say," we are told, "was, 'Charlie, just speak to me once.'" She returned to

Chicago, lost her mind, was committed to an insane asylum, and died a short time later.[35]

Nothing could stand in the way of the aggressive advance of the railroad, not the claims of the Native Americans, nor the resistance of nature, nor the dissoluteness and the distress of humans. Neither, finally, did massive corruption. To build so far-flung an enterprise as a transcontinental railroad, funds were required that far exceeded those available to any business or bank. Accordingly, entrepreneurs raised money through the sale of stocks and bonds, both here and in Europe. To assure themselves of a profit, no matter what would happen to the railroad, these same entrepreneurs set up construction businesses that contracted with the railroads. In their role of railroad magnates, they awarded themselves as contractors tens of millions of dollars in profits.[36] In the last two decades of the nineteenth century, the history of American railroads was one of financial and organizational collapse.[37] Yet people never concluded that the railroads simply might be creatures too unwieldy, cantankerous, and corruptible to bother with; collapse was invariably followed by reorganization and refinancing. The domination of nature required that distance and terrain, weather and season, be subdued. The aggressive attitude toward reality that propelled this conquest was so deeply entrenched that historians have described its advance as an obvious necessity, characterizing its violent progress as the sweetly reasonable demand for a transportation system that was "fast, cheap, and dependable," "year round in regularity, safe and cheap, overland and unlimited in route," providing "fast, all-weather transportation" and "safe, regular, reliable movement of goods and passengers."[38]

It would be ungenerous, however, to ignore the currents of constructive enthusiasm that ran beneath and between violence and corruption, rising occasionally to a grand and even selfless response to a majestic continent. Ralph Waldo Emerson, trying to discern and call forth the emerging American identity, saw in the land, especially in the "nervous [i.e., sinewy], rocky West," the force that would invigorate and calm the American character. He saw the railroad as the appropriate response to the vastness of the land, "a magician's rod, in its power to evoke the sleeping energies of land and water."[39]

Emerson's generous hopes were widely refracted in hackneyed

and embarrassing pronouncements about the triumphal procession of the Iron Horse, which would annihilate every obstacle, spreading sublime beauty as it raced along its earthshaking, fire-breathing path.[40] But Emerson was vindicated as well by people close to the ground. Stoyan Christowe left the war-torn Balkans early this century and began his American pilgrimage working on a section gang for the Montana Division of the Great Northern Railway. He was drawn by "the distant sorcery of the West, the freedom and mobility." "Broad, flat earth," he recalls from his journey west, "rolled away with American prodigality. And my being yearned to be one with it." In his view, building a railway on the American earth would not violate nature but adorn it: "The track ahead was but a thin stripe upon the earth's white expanse. And upon this band of steel the hundred men, like animated tumbleweeds, bent and twisted, bored and scratched. Upon the white bosom of American earth we engraved a necklace of steel—set in tie plates, clasped with bolts and angle bars, brocaded with spikes. And there it lay secured to the earth, immovable."[41] As Christowe touched the steel rails with his bare hands, he felt as though a candle had been lit inside him. "I had never," he exclaims, "felt so close to America as I did now in this pathless plain. I knew that as I touched the steel, linking one rail to another, I was linking myself to the new country and building my own solid road to a new life."[42]

To wrest commodious settlements from the wilderness was no mean endeavor. As Henry Bugbee reminds us, some of that constructive sentiment lives on in the opposition to setting aside wilderness areas.[43] It inflamed with all its youthful passion one of the heroes in Wallace Stegner's *Angle of Repose*. Constructive zeal endowed Oliver Ward with almost endless resourcefulness. It was not the harshness of the land that eventually brought Oliver to his knees but the fickleness of human affairs. Nor was it greed that fueled his persistence and ingenuity. He was, as his grandson muses, "in no race for wealth—that was precisely what disgusted Grandfather with the mining business. They were makers and doers, they wanted to take a piece of wilderness and turn it into a home for a civilization. I suppose they were wrong—their whole civilization was wrong—but they were the antithesis of mean or greedy."[44]

Wrong or not, that civilization—modern civilization—has come to its end. The Milwaukee Road used to span the continent and, taking its course across Montana, would run through Missoula and down along the Clark Fork. Today the Milwaukee is bankrupt; its line has been dismantled. The Northern Pacific had to merge with the Great Northern and the Burlington. But even this gigantic system found its southern line through Missoula burdensome and unprofitable and sold it to a local businessman. The major legacy that the Northern Pacific left to Missoula is a threat to its water supply. Since the 1950s, when locomotives were switched from steam to diesel, tens of thousands of gallons of fuel were spilled in the train yard. They soaked into the soil and now float on the water table. Pesticides, paint, and solvents are working their way down to the community's source of drinking water.[45]

Railroad building was not modernity's last assault on the American continent. In the late 1950s, the federal government embarked on the construction of the interstate highway system: I-90 now roughly parallels the railroads as it approaches and leaves Missoula. A four-lane, controlled-access highway is a much broader and more massive structure than a railroad. Hence highway construction was even more aggressively intrusive on the land than its railroad predecessors, even though it was gentler on the laborers, who benefited from heavy machinery and advanced logistics. At the same time, air traffic settled upon the country, and Missoula enlarged its airport to accommodate jets. While air traffic lanes are, of course, less tangible than railroads and highways, they have made transportation a ubiquitous presence on this continent. There is no refuge anywhere from the atmospheric and acoustic litter of airplanes. These feats of intrusion and construction are done and will not be repeated. Have we found, then, our angle of repose on this land?

METHODICAL UNIVERSALISM   In its initial stages, the campaign to subdue nature was a war of thousands of relatively limited and isolated forays. The spirit of domination was pervasive, yet its works were various and scattered. As the conquests grew and were consolidated, there was a need for large-scale integration. Baconian aggressiveness began to require the complement of Cartesian order. At length Cartesianism asserted itself through science and industry.

Science began to uncover and articulate the universal and lawful relations between heat and energy, between the pressure and volume of gases, and so illuminated, confirmed, and advanced rigorously what the inventions and improvements of the steam engines had accomplished intuitively or through trial and error.[46] In industry, too, Cartesian order emerged implicitly to fill the need for inclusive structures. This need arose from the magnitude and power of the Baconian efforts, which could no longer be contained by communal and traditional understandings. Resources were too precarious, machinery too expensive, production too abundant, transportation too extended, markets too fickle to be guided by intuitive appraisal, bonds of trust, and local adjustments. The modern response was the establishment of the rational, mechanical, and inclusive design we call the corporation.[47] Like the steam engine, the corporation emerged at the intersection of many lines, of exigency and ingenuity, of visionary schemes and incremental improvements. The history of the corporation is complex and irregular.[48] But, in retrospect, we can recognize in the resulting structure the pattern of the Cartesian method.

In the *Discourse on Method*, Descartes explicated his method in four rules: the rules of abstraction, of dissection, of reconstruction, and of control.[49] Faced with a problem, one must first abstract from it—step back from it and regard it from a skeptical distance. One also needs to abstract the problem itself—sever it from its context and our tacit understandings. Applying the rule to the organization of manufacture and commerce, one had to step outside unified and familiar arrangements and question the reach of personal and familial bonds, the efficacy of one person serving at once as the owner, operator, bookkeeper, and merchant of a business; one needed to examine the limits of providing for the traditional needs of well-known and immediate customers, the productivity of work that varied according to season, demand, and companionship.[50]

The second rule of Descartes's method requires that we dissect the problem before us into its simplest parts. Accordingly, the unified practice of the early modern economy had to be divided into several functions: legal counsel, treasurer, comptroller, purchasing agent, engineer, and so on.[51] The processes that could not be taken apart physically had to be analyzed conceptually through financial, statistical, and other analytic procedures, then rendered transparent in charts, graphs, accounts, ledgers, and files.

The third rule directs us to construct a new edifice from the several elements, proceeding from the simple to the complex.[52] In the corporate economy, the conceptually simple and guiding concept is the idea of rational organization, articulating itself more and more particularly from the superior to the more and more subordinate.[53] The shape that results is the hierarchy with the board of directors at the top and the laborers in the section gang at the bottom. The rational and mechanical functioning of such a structure is analogous to that of a machine.[54]

The fourth and final rule is to secure control over the region of concern through inclusiveness. In the corporate region, several dimensions must be controlled. The threat of competition was to be met horizontally through merger or acquisition; the uncertainty of resources and supply would be eliminated vertically through the inclusion of raw materials and supplier firms in the corporate structure. The wide vagaries of demand would be controlled through the incorporation of advertising and marketing mechanisms. Temporally, the fickleness of fate was to be reined in through research and development, long-range planning, and financial self-sufficiency.[55] The endless variety of local times was overcome through the establishment of standard time in four zones.[56] Most important, the corporation itself is a monument to time universal. Prior to its establishment, business enterprises would rise and fall with the fortunes of particular families or the temporary interests of partners. The corporation, to the contrary, is a legal person possessing eternal life.[57]

The corporation was modernism's response to the openness of the physical and social landscape of the New World. Through its methodical and inclusive organization, the corporation was able to mobilize and integrate the gigantic resources needed to conquer a presumably wide-open continent. At the same time, the corporation gave cohesion and identity to a mass of individuals who had left their communities behind and had grown impatient with establishing new ones. In Europe, where communities had been and remained in place, modern technology was sometimes developed in more flexible and de-centralized ways, coordinated by shared understandings and mutual support.[58] In the United States, the most sophisticated and sustained efforts at stabilizing the railroad industry through cooperative agreements came to naught.[59]

The genius of the corporation is its fusion of humanity and technology, of individual aspiration and giant machinery. This genius is well expressed in the corporate line and staff organization where the entire responsibility for a well-defined and coherent part of a corporation is entrusted to one individual. The person in a line position, aided by a staff, occupies a place in the corporate hierarchy *and* has broad control over his or her particular realm.[60] At the same time, the individual has a prospect of rising in the hierarchy and commanding an ever more inclusive portion of it. In this way, the individuals identify themselves with the corporation and in turn elaborate its identity through their individual efforts. This fusion is most intense among the managers in the higher echelons of the corporate hierarchy and diminishes in strength lower down among the laborers as well as higher up among directors and stockholders.[61] The great corporations have been a pervasive force of social integration in American society. Their success is evident from their share in this country's economy. Although they constitute less than a tenth of a percent of all firms, they control half of the total economy.[62]

The historical aptness and massive appearance of the corporation has made it seem as though the corporate structure has been the outcome of an iron and rational necessity, as though the modern project was realizable in this form exclusively. But this is a modern conceit. The industrial economy might have been organized quite differently.[63] At any rate, as we near the postmodern divide, the corporate structure is weakening and receding. What once was a framework for individual identity is now itself suffering an identity crisis.[64]

AMBIGUOUS INDIVIDUALISM   When divinity and monarchy were questioned as the grounds of the common order at the transition to the modern era, Locke advanced the sovereignty of the individual as the fundament of authority. While the Baconian and Cartesian bequests to modernity are fairly straightforward forces, Lockean individualism has always been a tangled affair.

Individualism serves Locke as a powerful instrument to criticize the old order. But how do we get from separate and autonomous individuals to an inclusive and binding commonwealth? To answer this question Locke appeals to a broadly conceived power whose vagueness is apparent from the variety of its names: state of nature, law of nature, law of reason.[65] The political incompleteness of the individual and the ambiguity of the compensating force have made individualism a troublesome concept ever since.

The word "individual" is rarely found in Locke's vocabulary; "individualism" is not found at all. Locke usually speaks of "every one" or "every man." The word "individualism" was coined by Alexis de Tocqueville, who found it forced upon him when he investigated American democracy in the early nineteenth century.[66] Incompleteness and ambiguity did not hinder the progress of individualism, however. In fact, the individual at first appears to be the natural complement to the execution of the modern project. The individual is the author of the enterprise and the beneficiary of its fruits.[67] The former of these two functions has been fixed in the American consciousness as rugged individualism; the latter leads a more surreptitious life in commodity consumption. I will call this second function commodious individualism.

With all its prominence, so evident to Tocqueville, American individualism has failed to escape ambiguity. Not only does rugged individualism, fondly and frequently invoked in the life of this nation, have a softer commodious sibling; rather both rugged and commodious individualism at once reveal and conceal the character of the modern project, particulary in its American realization. Nor is this the end of ambiguity. Each resolved strand seems to unravel and call for further and endless divisions.

The image of the rugged individual conjures up people who, facing up to a wild continent, were provoked to superhuman feats of ingenuity and endurance and bespoke in their weathered faces and plain behavior the grandeur of the land they had prevailed against. Edward Gilette the surveyor, J. L. Hallett the engineer, James H. Kyner the contractor, Stoyan Christowe the laborer—all were rugged individuals. Without them, the modern project would not have proceeded so vigorously and rapidly on this continent.

Clearly, too, the children of these rugged individuals have inherited commodious freedom in the ways they prefer to shape their private lives—above all the freedom to move about, nearly at will. In 1889, Josiah Royce, then a professor at Harvard, was asked "to describe some of the principal physical aspects of California, and to indicate the way in which they have been related to the life and civilization of the region." Royce could think of no better way of guiding his listeners' attention than to take them on a mental journey from the Mississippi to the Pacific coast. Naturally, it was a railroad trip, and what impressed Royce deeply was its ease and speed: "The region that to-day is so swiftly and so easily entered was of old the goal of an overland tour that might easily last six months from the Missouri River, and that was attended with many often-recorded dangers." [68]

Since then, mobility and commodity have increased much further. Today few would consider a two- or three-day train ride swift and easy when a jet will get us there in a matter of hours. Meanwhile, too, commodiousness is not just ease in traversing space but unencumbered movement in the social sphere. The heirs of rugged individualism take it for granted that they are free to marry or not, to have children whether they are or are not married, and to go their separate ways if they no longer want to be together. If they are of Norwegian descent but have a taste for Italian culture, they can turn to pizza, Pavarotti, and *La Strada*. If they dislike their Protestant upbringing, they may move to Catholicism or Buddhism.

We already know from the corporate implementation of Cartesian universalism that the individualist account of modernity is one-sided. Though corporations were often founded and structured by outstanding individuals, the corporation in its mature form transforms individuals into anonymous managers and workers. Modern common sense seems to concede the limits of individualism and distinguishes between the private and the public, between the sphere of individual discretion and the sphere of collective regimentation. But far from delimiting and clarifying individualism, the public–private distinction is itself an almost artfully complex confusion of the question where to locate authority and responsibility in the modern project. To begin with, there are two divergent distinctions between the public and the private; we may call them the economic distinction and the social distinction. Each designates an area for the exercise of individualism. The social distinction delimits the private realm as the sphere of commodious individualism; the economic distinction marks out the private sector as the field where rugged individualism will prosper. As it turns out, in fact, the social distinction serves to conceal the debilities of commodious individualism while the economic distinction exploits rugged individualism to justify the violence and injustice of the modern economy.

The social distinction has its origin in the ancient difference between the intimacy and seclusion of family life and the more open and inclusive life of the community.[69] Before the modern period this was a supple division. Life shifted easily in the regular rhythm of seasons and celebrations from the familial to the communal and back again. In the common recollection of European culture, the village community designated the local boundaries of this life, the church provided its center, and nobility constituted its authority. Our common aspirations are haunted to this day by the surveyable and personal life in the village community and by the focused and festive splendor of religious and feudal celebrations.[70] We have similar remembrances of Athens and the Roman republic.

At no point was the organic texture of public and private life in the Middle Ages rent abruptly and entirely. Strands of it have survived to this day. But it did unravel gradually in the fire of the cultural and political conflagrations of the early modern period. Industrialism, the legacy of Bacon's vision, began to destroy the substance of village life; the Enlightenment, the program of Descartes and Locke, began to supersede the cultural authority of church and nobility.

A new configuration of public and private life emerged in the London and Paris of the eighteenth century. The chief actor in this life was the newly prosperous and confident bourgeoisie. Its members were able to step out of the privacy of their homes into a realm of artful public celebration, marked by stylized dress and speech, enacted in parks and streets, in theaters and coffeehouses.[71] But for this achievement, the bourgeoisie borrowed heavily from the cultural treasures of the *ancien régime*. The challenge never met was a harmony of public and private life that would be democratic and modern.

The American continent, of course, never wore the fabric of medieval life, yet the early settlers brought late medieval practices and institutions with them. In many instances, the hardness of pioneer life and the hurriedness of conquering the land prevented people from recreating the communal charms of the Old World in the New World. But in even the roughest and freshest settlements of the West, settlers joined at once to erect a school and a church, powerful focuses of common life.

In the nineteenth century, however, the organic interchange of the public and the private came under stress and was finally destroyed. Destruction came in the guise of ostentation. This was the time when department stores, libraries, and opera houses were erected as magnificent settings in which the public could gather and enjoy itself. But the people who filled these spaces had become silent, passive, and distracted. No longer actors and connoisseurs of public spectacles, they had begun to turn into recipients and consumers of commodities, produced for them by experts.[72]

The railroad companies played a central role in the transformation of the common order. They built the most imposing public structures—both the widely spreading network of lines and the massive and luxurious stations. Grand Central Station in New York City became the emblem of the gathering and convergence of thousands of people and hundreds of facilities. It became a symbol, too, of architectural magnificence.[73]

Some such presence was to be found in every town, no matter how small. More accurately, the presence of a railroad depot was the condition of survival for just about every town on this continent. The railroad not only brought commercial prosperity; it also sucked the life from the rural culture beyond its lines. In towns served by a railroad, the depot became a center of curiosity and entertainment. It rivaled school, church, and city center as the central point of public life.[74]

The conviviality of the railroad station lacked a substantial center, however. Its chief purpose, after all, was instrumental; it was transportation, not celebration. As faster or more flexible means of transportation became available, the railroads and their stations were deserted.[75] The decay of these signal structures of common life after the Second World War might have alerted the nation to the disturbed and unsettled balance of public and private life, but the issue was buried under a transformation of common living space even swifter and more radical than the building of the railroads. Interstate highways reshaped life horizontally, high rises vertically.

These constructions surpassed the railroads in both their physical mass and their dedication to the instrumental. As engineering feats, they dominate, if they do not suffocate, public space. If we do not admire them, they nontheless overwhelm our attention. Yet their reason for being is entirely that of a means—means of moving and storage. Thus the public realm of the late twentieth-century United States has become both hypertrophied and atrophied, both excessively developed in its sheer physical presence and devoid of intrinsic or final dignity, bereft of celebration and festivity.[76]

The late modern luxuriance of the public realm has all but overgrown the private realm. And yet, since the public realm is ostensibly instrumental, it requires the private realm of leisure and consumption as its final complement. Privacy now serves as a term to designate the essence of the private realm. Its idiosyncrasy emerges most clearly in its legal setting. We think of privacy today as both eminently desirable and frequently threatened. This tension has led naturally to litigation and to the Supreme Court. But privacy is not mentioned explicitly in the Constitution. To protect privacy, the Court had to search the penumbra of the Bill of Rights for grounds to do so.[77]

There is not only a problem of saying why privacy should be protected, there is the prior difficulty of saying what privacy is and what constitutes a violation of it. Surely privacy is different from autonomy or personal liberty. For it is possible to grant someone freedom in all personal regards and yet invade his or her privacy through snooping or eavesdropping. Nor is just any intrusion of the personal realm a violation of privacy. Some, such as unwanted noises or odors, are merely nuisances.[78]

Reasoning along these lines, Thomas Huff has isolated the notion of privacy as freedom from intrusions that can lead to an unwarranted judgment on the person whose sphere of intimacy has been invaded.

Of course, our next of kin, who are naturally members of our personal circle, and friends whom we have invited into it are entitled to judge whatever we do. But no one else may do so without our permission.[79]

Such a notion of privacy would have remained limited and uninteresting in a premodern setting where the contextual nature of work and celebration was mirrored in a greater continuity of family and community. Families identified themselves with the moral standards of the community; they depended on communal cooperation for entertainment and celebration. But with the rise and progressive articulation of modern prosperity and liberty, these communal ties came to be seen as burdens and have since been removed to make room for commodious individualism, the unencumbered enjoyment of consumption goods or commodities. What Huff calls the privacy norm is in large part the collective affirmation of consumption as an exercise of freedom that would be encumbered by judgmental intrusion. Intrusion by whom? Huff speaks of the private realm as "that part of our lives conducted with families and friends."[80] But we increasingly withdraw from the judgments of our friends, parents, and spouses. At the limit, the realm of privacy is in each case occupied by one consumer.

We are steadily moving toward that limit and in the process have transformed our environment and our habits. The transformation of our surroundings came into focus in 1986 when the Consumer Union, looking back on fifty years of publishing *Consumer Reports,* selected from the hundred thousand or so products and services reviewed in its journal those fifty that "revolutionized our lives."[81] What first appears to be a great variety of items turns out to sort comfortably into four categories: comfort and convenience items (15), health and safety items (13), transportation items (11), entertainment items (8), and education items (3). Their collective effect is to remove or ease the burdens of life that formerly would direct us to our family and community for aid and solace, to give us individual mobility in the pursuit of our ends, and to procure for unencumbered enjoyment the riches of entertainment. This is evident enough from the first ten items in the alphabetical listing:

air conditioners
air travel

antibiotics
Austin/Morris Mini 1959
automatic transmission
black and white T.V.
color T.V.
compact discs
credit cards
detergents

Individualism also shows itself in the daily habits that correspond to this increasingly commodious setting. It is most clearly reflected in the ways we spend the time that is exclusively ours, our leisure. Leisure is the time that is left when our work is done, our children are cared for, we have attended to our personal and educational needs, after we have served our organizations and entertained our friends. Considering its development within the last generation, we find that from 1965 to 1975 leisure grew by ten percent to somewhere between twenty-eight and twenty-nine hours per week.[82] Of our waking hours, leisure occupies the largest share, more than paid work (on the average about twenty-six hours per week), household chores (fifteen hours), and everything else (twenty-one hours), excepting personal care (seventy-eight hours, including sleep).[83]

Eighty percent of leisure is passive consumption; being passive, it is essentially solitary.[84] Television comprises sixty percent of it, and the lure of its commodious privacy increasingly has drawn the more skilled and educated among us as well.[85] Such activities as listening to music and reading, which are intrinsically as private as television watching, account for most of the remaining passive leisure.[86] Only our two hours of conversation per week constitute passive and communal leisure.[87]

In leisure, individualism seems to be close to the extreme privacy Tocqueville foresaw more than a century and a half ago. Here individualism throws one "back forever upon himself alone and threatens in the end to confine him entirely within the solitude of his own heart."[88] But we have artfully concealed the desolation of this solitude behind the massive ostentation of the public realm and under the judicial elaboration of privacy. Ironically, just when commodious individualism seems reduced to its final undividedness and protected from common scrutiny, new doubts and divisions open up. It appears that people enjoy least what they indulge in most. Generally they find activities without personal interaction unsatisfying. And television in particular is thought to have little intrinsic benefit.[89] In fact, during the very decade that television watching increased so substantially, television boycotting rose, too.[90]

Since 1975, passive leisure appears not to have grown and work time not to have shrunk further. In fact television viewing has diminished a little, and interactive leisure and conversations, at least on the telephone, have increased.[91] But the overall picture has not changed. Commodious privacy remains both strong and unloved. Work, however, the descendant of rugged individualism, appears to be well regarded.[92]

That seems natural enough. Work is hard, serious, and constructive; leisure is certainly commodious, perhaps frivolous if not parasitic. To work is to be vigorously in touch with reality; it is to acquire substance and property. Of the worker Locke says: "Whatsoever, then, he removes out of the state that nature hath provided and left it in, he hath mixed his labour with, and joined to it something that is his own, and thereby makes it his property." The working man and the working woman are entitled to reward and respect. God, Locke says (he might as well have said nature or reason), gave the world "to the use of the industrious and rational (and labour was to be his title to it), not to the fancy or covetousness of the quarrelsome and contentious." As we understand him, Locke is speaking of rugged individuals, finding fulfillment in the conquest of an untamed continent. America is the paradigm of the world in the state of nature, presented to humans as an opportunity and a task, for, Locke tells us, "in the beginning all the world was America."[93]

The fruits that the individuals gather from nature through their work become, as Locke has it, their "private right," possessed "for their private uses."[94] To guard the individuals' unencumbered exercise of industry and their enjoyment of the fruits of their labors, this country has been zealous in marking out and protecting an extensive private sector for individual economic endeavors.

This brings us to the economic public–private distinction. Obviously, it does not coincide with the social distinction. If we agree to call the areas distinguished by the social division "realms" and those distinguished by the economic division "sectors," we can say simply that most of the private sector is in the public realm. The private sector is out in the open, collectively inhabited, and heavily regimented—far removed from the Lockean idyll. Especially of late, the private sector seems to reward prodigiously "the fancy or covetousness of the quarrelsome and contentious."

The private sector is hospitable neither to self-determination nor to a vigorous engagement with nature. Young people do not look to the labor market as a field for creative self-realization. Instead, they look for available slots in the gigantic economic machinery to insert their labor. They do so anxiously if they are ambitious, sullenly when they are hopeless. Once they have found work, what they confront is not the challenge of soil, rock, or timber, but the incessant demands of technological devices, impersonal supervisors, and anonymous customers. They certainly find no natural balance between the industry and rationality of their work and the rewards of their labor.

Why, then, do we persist in extolling and defending the private sector? To find an answer we must consider more closely the line that divides the private from the public sector. Conventionally, the public sector is' thought to consist of three parts. First, there is the government with its machinery, the bureaucracy and the personnel that immediately serve the three branches of government as they design and enact public policy. Second, there are certain means of producing goods and services that belong to the state, such as timber and grazing lands, the educational system, the national weather service, and so on. Finally, there is the hybrid part composed of those social resources that are collected and spent by the government for the public good through private enterprise, for example, the tax funds given to private construction firms to build or maintain highways, to produce weapons, or to reforest public lands. The rest of the economy constitutes the private sector.

The line between the public and private sectors is drawn differently in different countries. In European countries, the railroads are on the public side of the divide while in this country they belong to the private sector. And though our railroads are private, they would not have developed as quickly and widely as they did without public support.[95] Today the government heavily controls the welfare of the railroads through legislation—determining taxes, financial transactions, working conditions, environmental impacts, rates, and comparative advantages or burdens assigned to competing forms of transportation.

These remarks illustrate a broader thesis put forward by John Kenneth Galbraith in 1967 to the effect that in the new industrial state, government, business, the unions, the educational and scientific estate form but one coherent system.[96] This is not to say, of course, that the new industrial system fails to have functionally distinct parts or that it is not important to keep those parts distinct. Rather, it is to point out that our sharply drawn and zealously guarded line between the public and private sectors is unilluminating and confusing from the technical and technological point of view.

Why are we so zealous, then, about the private sector? We persist in designating a large part of the economy as private so that we can disavow public responsibility for its evils and claim individual merit for its blessings. As a civic body, we are reluctant to countenance and cure the deprivations of the poor, the damage to the environment, and the trivialization of culture that are the depressing concomitants of our advanced industrial economy. At the same time, applauding the rich and powerful who claim their privileges as the fruits of their rugged and individual efforts, we sanction our positions or our aspirations.

The festering ambiguities of individualism, though they have been culturally and morally injurious, remained politically and economically tolerable as long as the economy was productive and consumption was moderate. But lately, commodious individualism has become unbridled. At the same time, the rugged individualists' insistence on splitting apart what can only prosper through cooperation is slowing the economy and putting it, in a historical and international perspective, at a troubling disadvantage. Individualism has always been ambiguous. Now, at last, it is becoming questionable.

3. POSTMODERNISM

Postmodernism is a wide and colorful movement. It is not my purpose to survey and classify it.[1] I use the term to mark the emerging divide between two epochs. Among the authors from whom I have learned to recognize this watershed, some would welcome the postmodernist label for their work and others would be offended by such an appellation. What matters for my purposes is that they have helped to shed light on the end of one era and the beginning of another.

An epoch approaches its end when its fundamental conviction begins to weaken and no longer inspires enthusiasm among its advocates. That is true of each of the three parts of the modern project: realism, universalism, and individualism. I have traced this program chiefly in its social and economic setting. Yet modernism was an intellectual and artistic enterprise as well. To see the decline of modernity in its entirety, we must consider these aspects, however briefly, both their programmatic formulations and the criticisms that have been levied against them.

The intellectual enterprise needs no introduction. Throughout the discussion of modernism I have used the thought of philosophers to construct a framework for my account of modernism. In doing so, I have recognized the seismographic significance of modern philosophy. To be sure, philosophers sometimes think of their work more grandly as having the kind of earthshaking power that levels the haphazard and untidy structures of the past and of possessing the kind of fundamental authority that lays down the principles for the construction of a better world.

Though this is surely a delusion, philosophy has always been an important voice in the conversation of humanity. The claims and criticisms of philosophy do shore up and weaken, reveal and conceal in various ways, the structures and aspirations of the common order. So one should recognize that philosophy has had some practical force in the formulation and execution of the modern project. Moreover, if its seismographic significance was helpful for reading the tremors that announced the shaping of the modern period, it may help us again in deciphering the decline of modernity.

What happened within modern philosophy is a more radical version of the economic enterprise whose crucial features philosophy aids us in registering. To reorganize the realm of thought is not merely to conquer and to rearrange but to raze and level entirely, and to rebuild from the ground up. Descartes was the first to conceive of this project. Mainstream modern philosophy from Descartes to the middle of this century has been nothing but a series of proposals, each attempting to outdo the other in the radicality of its revolutionary destruction and in the cogency of its enlightened reconstruction.

Philosophers have been thinking of these endeavors not as revisions of their professional games but as transformations of the real world. They have thought of thinking as the matrix of reality. To reformulate thinking, then, was to establish once and for all what henceforth would count as real and what would not. To make reality subject to the dictates of the philosopher is to pursue aggressive realism by other means, more radical and less consequential means as it turned out. Radicality is apparent in the endeavor to accomplish across the board and for all time what miners, settlers, and railroad builders undertook here and there and for the time being. It is evident in the philosophers' claim that once they had subdued reality to their standards of validity, every human enterprise would have to take its measures of reality from philosophy.[2]

Very few did, in fact. Specific philosophical programs remained inconsequential for the most part. Outsiders could hardly fail to notice that, although the general modern program was pursued zealously by nearly all philosophers, no particular realization of it ever gained the consensus of the profession. Yet the revolutionary vigor of the modern temper sustained the philosophical project. Philosophers invariably reacted to failure with new attempts, fueled by the determination to succeed through greater circumspection and incisiveness where preceding efforts had foundered.

Failure overtook modern philosophy regularly at its constructive turn. The idea was to rebuild the edifice of thought with indisputably solid materials. But the building blocks all turned out to be flawed in this way or that. For Descartes, the ego was to be the cornerstone of reconstruction. But doubts were soon raised, and have been ever since, whether the ego has the indubitable solidity that Descartes claimed for it and, even if it did, whether it could serve as the beginning for the rational reconstruction of reality.

Criticism was crucial in propelling modern philosophy from project to project. But it was always piecemeal and destructive, designed as an explosive charge to clear away the specific claims of a particular predecessor. It was not until the second half of this century that the coherence of these criticisms began to emerge and with them the beginnings of an alternative to the very idea of modern philosophy. The decisive synoptic achievement belongs to Richard Rorty, who carefully and resourcefully went through many of the major modern projects and showed that whatever was advanced as cogent and fundamental was invariably undergirded by a contestable agreement of a community of speakers.[3]

Thus Descartes, in advancing the ego and consciousness as the unshakable foundation for the enlightened reconstruction of reality, responded to the unsettled culture of his day and sought to persuade his readers to agree on the need for an indubitable mooring in the stormy seas of scientific revolutions and religious wars.[4] But once we recognize indubitable rigor as the doubtful rigidity of a particular agreement, we are ready to countenance other conventions that allow for a human conversation of many voices.

Rorty entitled the concluding section of his book *Philosophy and the Mirror of Nature* "Philosophy in the Conversation of Mankind." He explained his choice, saying, "I end this book with an allusion to Oakeshott's famous title, because it catches the tone in which, I think, philosophy should be discussed."[5] This title captures the tone of modern philosophy all too well since women were excluded from the modern conversation, although Rorty certainly did not intend to exclude them from the postmodern conversation.[6] But his slip of the pen, if not of sensibility, does provide a clue to the unreal character of postmodern philosophy.

Though Rorty in his recent writings gladly admits the female voice to the conversation of humanity, his remains a strictly human conversation. As Rorty has it, "people discourse whereas things do not." Nature is utterly silent for Rorty and speaks only by the grace of human conventions and concessions, for "nature has no preferred way of being represented."[7] Rorty opposes not just aggressive realism but any realism that recognizes the eloquence of things. When a postmodern theorist makes that claim in a windowless lecture hall containing hundreds of humans, speaking up on behalf of the voices silenced by the auditorium walls requires more sensitivity and courage than most of us can muster. As it turns out, allowing women to enter the conversation does not merely enrich its tonal color but gives real weight to its content as well.

Joan Rothschild's anthology *Machina ex Dea*, too, is a critique of modern aggressive realism.[8] Yet it is more than an indictment of the largely inconsequential endeavors of philosophers. It exposes the violence and cruelty of the modern project. What one learns from Rothschild's collection is that the modern project is not simply the advancement of an age-old human striving for more comfort and security but the mobilization of a peculiar masculine aggressiveness that breaks through ancient restraints and reserves.[9] One also learns from *Machina ex Dea* that the modern advances in disburdening and enriching daily life were of ambiguous value to women. They eased the burden of housework, but they also eroded its social and economic substance and dissolved its communal context. They liberated and enervated at the same time.[10] What Rothschild's collection points up is the conjunction of violence and vacuity that characterizes the modern relation to reality. There is the violent clash of the modern project with nature and community, and in its wake, wherever under favored conditions modern tranquillity attains its paradigmatic shape, there is vacuity as the force and presence of reality seem to evaporate.

Of Universalism Aggressive realism, we should remember, was not entirely wanton aggression. It was in part a constructive reply to the disintegration of the medieval order. The loss of cohesion and orientation was not only an invitation to reorder physical and philosophical reality; it was also a challenge to human conduct. What got lost along with the village community and the central position of the church were the habits of rural life and the celebration of Christian sacraments that served as moral landmarks in the daily round of life. Once these points of orientation had been shattered or obscured, a new method was needed to find one's way, something like a compass, a universal instrument of moral navigation that would work regardless of one's particular circumstances. In this spirit Descartes in his *Discourse on Method* sought "Some Moral Rules Derived from the Method."[11] Descartes's rules are evidently a response to the disorientation he felt, yet they only go part way toward devising a reliable universal instrument, reflecting a mixture of cautious acquiescence and shrewd planning.

The project of devising a universal moral compass came into its own in Kant's 1785 *Foundations of the Metaphysics of Morals*.[12] For Kant, particular circumstances and motives are unsuitable for moral guidance almost by definition. This particular situation may suggest honesty as the best course of action, and my inclination at the moment may be high-minded and forthright. But who can guarantee that next time around circumstances may not counsel subterfuge and my attitude may not be one of diffidence?

Kant responded by calling for a law of human conduct that would hold regardless of particular conditions—an unconditional, categorical imperative. And with an ingenious sleight of thought, Kant declared the purely opposite of the particular and contingent, namely, universality, to be the necessary and sufficient foundation of moral conduct. "Act universally," says the categorical imperative. More explicitly it says: "Act only according to that maxim by which you can at the same time will that it should become a universal law."[13]

This is the law that human reason gives to itself. Since everyone is endowed with reason, every individual is both a lawgiver and a subordinate in the moral realm. Reasoning thus, Kant yoked individualism and universalism together, supplying a foundation for liberal democratic theory and its ideals of autonomy and equality. These ideals constitute both the precious bequest and the unfinished agenda of the modern project. It is obvious, however, that modernism has spent its energy and is now unable to realize autonomy and equality through its own resources and according to its own conceptions.

It was soon replied to Kant that he had purchased universality at the price of vacuity, that the categorical imperative without tacit support of particular circumstances and agreements tells you nothing of consequence.[14] One remarkable attempt at rehabilitating the Kantian project is that of Lawrence Kohlberg. His idea is to reconcile the universal with the particular by tracing the emergence of the ethically universal attitude in the particular stages of moral development. That moral maturing, moreover, is taken to be an ascent from the subordination to particular and heteronomous forces to the freedom of universal ethical principles. More particularly, Kohlberg describes moral development as beginning in infancy when a child's conduct is shaped by the rule of a superior authority. Gradually a person comes to recognize that others can be bargained with, that their concerns can be shared and guarded, that there is a social order undergirding individual concerns, that this order in turn is based on fundamental rights, and, finally, that basic values derive from "universal ethical principles that all humanity should follow."[15]

Kohlberg articulated this development in six stages and attempted to show through empirical investigation that human moral development in fact passes through these stages.[16] Everyone, Kohlberg claimed, sets out on this path of development, though not everyone reaches its endpoint. "Prominent among those who thus appear to be deficient in moral development when measured by Kohlberg's scale," says Carol Gilligan, "are women whose judgments seem to exemplify the third stage of his six-stage sequence."[17] Here one is "concerned about the other people and their feelings, keeping loyalty and trust with partners"; one is "aware of shared feelings, agreements, and expectations, which take primacy over individual interests."[18]

Gilligan agrees that these concerns and attitudes characterize women's moral conduct, yet she disagrees that this represents a lower or less mature kind of moral life. In her own investigations, Gilligan found that women are bearers of a morality that is distinguished from the reigning masculine morality of universal rights and principles. While she is guarded about the roots and causes of this distinction, Gilligan stresses the fact that women in their moral conduct put relationships above rules, care above justice, and intimacy above the quest for individual identity.

Gilligan's book is a monument in feminism. At the same time it is a crucial document in the critique of modernist universalism, because more prominently than any other essay it has shown the universal to be particular. Moral universalism is just a particular way of arranging the common order and recognizing shortcomings and merits within it. It is an arrangement that favors appropriation through formal and abstract intelligence and implementation through the subordination of the particular to some universal measure.

A focal point of the contention between the masculine and feminine moral voice is the dilemma Kohlberg poses about the man named Heinz whose wife is mortally ill and needs an expensive drug Heinz cannot afford, but the druggist will not sell for less. What is Heinz to do? The masculine way is to reach for the universal principle, to loosen it upon the case at hand and see the solution drop out. Let the principle be that life comes before property. It follows that Heinz should steal the drug.

The feminine approach is to immerse oneself in the particularity of the task, to consider the consequences that stealing would have on the life of Heinz and his wife, to explore alternatives to stealing like borrowing the money or seeking an understanding between Heinz and the druggist.[19] Universalism neglects these ways of empathy and care and is harsh toward the human subtleties and frailties that do not convert into the universal currency.

"Dominance" is Michael Walzer's term for a social arrangement where one kind of good is the measure of all other things, be it money, education, or birthright. If you possess the dominant good in abundance, you can command most other goods through exchange.[20] If the dominant good is concentrated in the hands of a few, Walzer calls the arrangement "monopoly." In light of these definitions, Gilligan's critique can be described as a challenge to the dominance of modern masculine morality, its exclusive claim on determining moral significance. The challenges within modern morality, to the contrary, have chiefly been to monopoly, to the accumulation of moral authority, not to the particular quality of moral authority.

The major liability of moral universalism is its dominance; the consequence of dominance is an oppressive impoverishment of moral life. While Gilligan has made the major breach in the wall of universalism and dominance, Walzer has shown that the wall has many sections in addition to the moral one, and that each is a barrier to a rich and vital community. More particularly, Walzer has argued that the common order is composed of a variety of major goods, each requiring its particular appreciation and assignment. The measure of distribution for welfare is need; for education it is talent; for honor, merit; for political power, leadership.

Universalism has been dethroned in almost every field of contemporary culture, from mathematics, by way of physics and biology to anthropology, the law, and literature.[21] It is now seen as an anxious and pretentious yet ultimately futile effort to enforce rigor and uniformity in an unruly and luxuriant world.

Of Individualism   In the conversation of scholars, universalism may have been revealed to be an emperor without clothes, but in the practical affairs of this country, universalism armed with technological aggressiveness has been an awful force. Rugged individuals have led and cheered it on, but not all people on this continent rode the crest or followed the wake of individualism. Some of them had lived here as members of ancient communities. The progress of universally powerful machines and procedures broke into their lives first as an ominous rumble and then as a devastating flood.

In Louise Erdrich's *Love Medicine,* we see the destruction that has been left behind.[22] The Native Americans feel fear or contempt toward rugged individuals and live at the outer margins of commodious individualism. Gerry Nanapush takes on a cowboy who calls him a nigger. From then on, this man, destined by gifts of body and mind to be a leader of his people, is condemned to a fugitive life. Gerry's half brother, Henry Lamartine, Jr., returns from Vietnam disoriented and inconsolate; he finally drowns himself. King Kapshaw, half brother to Gerry's son, is given to alcoholism and violent outbursts; he ends up stupefied and isolated in the Twin Cities. King's father, Gordie, entirely succumbs to alcohol and is sent to a rehabilitation center.

Gerry's legal father, Henry Lamartine, in error or distress drives his car into the path of a train.

These people in northern North Dakota are presented to us in fourteen fragmentary episodes reflecting their broken lives. When their communal bonds are shattered, the men particularly drift into desolation and death. June Kapshaw, too, the woman who bore Gerry and Gordie sons, in the very first episode of the book finds herself half undressed and stretched out on the seat of a pickup beneath a drunk oilfield worker who had passed out. She opens the door, falls out of the truck, and gathers herself up to walk home across the prairie and through a spring snow storm. She, too, dies. Yet Erdrich concludes the episode by saying, "The snow fell deeper that Easter than it had in forty years, but June walked over it like water and came home."[23] After her degrading final encounter with the white man, June came home because she had begun to free and cleanse herself of degradation. She ended her life purely out on the plains in the snow.

The world that was overlaid by the white man's culture could not provide a home for her fierce and graceful beauty. But the world of the Kapshaws and Lamartines does not surrender completely to the devastations and temptations of commodious individualism. As the fragments of Erdrich's book accumulate, relations begin to emerge like a vascular system fighting for its life. At the heart of the system are women who have the power to forgive and endure, two matriarchs in particular. Marie Kapshaw and Lulu Lamartine for much of the time vie for the affection of the gifted but uncertain Nector, Marie's husband and Lulu's lover. In the end, Nector fades into senility and death. Marie and Lulu join forces. Lipsha, their common relative, recovers and carries on the love medicine of his tradition. His most trusted cousin, Albertine, goes to medical school.

The stirrings of life and health remain feeble and imperiled among the Native Americans of Erdrich's book. After all, the modern project has fractured their communities and rituals, their dwellings and their crafts, their stories and their dances, their loyalties and their divinities. Exactly the same must be said, however, of the white premodern culture. It, too, has lost its habits of the heart. There is an enormous difference, of course. Among the white people, the modern project arose gradually, supported by a great deal of consensus or at least complicity.

The Native Americans encountered it as a sudden and detested devastation. This difference has long concealed the cultural destruction that modern individualism has worked on its own ancestry.

The concealment was lifted when, in 1985, Robert Bellah, Richard Madsen, William Sullivan, Ann Swidler, and Steven Tipton published *Habits of the Heart: Individualism and Commitment in American Life.* They looked into the lives of the people who were the paradigmatic beneficiaries of the modern project, America's prosperous middle class. What they found is a glamorous and complicitous enactment of the destitute and oppressive conditions Erdrich depicts. These white folks, too, leave their home, become spiritually lost, are deprived of good work, seek refuge in illusory realms, fall prey to frivolous seductions, and forsake love's medicine for the anesthesia of therapy.[24]

These losses, as the authors recognize, are commonly covered up by the commodious surface of middle-class life and by the myths of self-reliance and heroic individualism.[25] It is the recollection of alternative forces, of the republican and biblical traditions, that allows Bellah and his coauthors to uncover the ravages of individualism. What lays our common wounds bare also holds out a promise of regeneration. Communities of memory and practices of commitment still have animating power at the margins of society.[26] These we must learn to recover and to respect.

Universalism in the cultural debate of the modern period for the most part stood in the background as the unquestionable and often invisible authority. When it moved to the center of critical attention, its fall from power was precipitous. Individualism, having been elusive all along, turns out to be elastic under criticism. It certainly has not been shattered and replaced by *Habits of the Heart,* but the extraordinarily wide and warm reception the book has received is testimony that individualism has become questionable.

Of Architecture In modern architecture, splendor and squalor arose side by side. The factories and tenement blocks of the late nineteenth century were massive, dark, and dirty. At the same time, schools, libraries, museums, opera houses, theaters, railroad stations, and churches were erected in the grand styles that meant to appropriate the magnificence of traditional edifices for public pleasure and enlightenment. The cities that came into being were forever struggling to achieve a measure of balance and harmony as they wrestled with the water supply, attempted to dispose of wastes, were choking in throngs of horse-drawn vehicles, hemmed in by hundreds of overhead telephone lines, and engulfed with soot from countless coal fires. The cities were still medieval in their messy vitality and diversity.

They became truly modern through the catalysis of the automobile.[27] Architects and city planners never favored the car, yet they found its modern logic irresistible. The passenger car, if anything, allowed the individual to conquer time and space by means of a universal device. Thus the automobile became the vehicle of modernism, the force that empowered builders to reorder the untidy and irrational structures of the late nineteenth and early twentieth centuries.

Since classical antiquity, streets and city blocks had patterned the fabric of urban life. The street had always been a complex of functions: living space, playground, stage, workshop, bazaar, transportation link. Such ill-defined complexity offended the modern intellect at the outset and eventually was overtaxed and upset by automobile traffic.[28] This gave architects license to tear up and discard the traditional urban fabric and to replace it with freestanding high rises at the center and with endless suburbia in its surroundings. The various parts were to be connected by limited-access expressways.[29]

The assault of the modern project on the urban setting displayed the ruthless zeal of a frustrated revolutionary parent. In this instance, modernism did not set out to raze ancient traditions or conquer untamed nature; it turned upon its firstborn children, the cities that had grown up as modern creatures but had failed to measure up to the standards of a rational and enlightened order.[30] Thus the aggressive realism that once had cleared forests and dynamited mountains now used dynamite to clear slums and excavate canyons for expressways. The open spaces were filled with a design that displayed its modern and universal force in its very name, the Modern or International Style.[31] The results were of rigorously Cartesian purity, realizations of a three-dimensional coordinate system, where orientation was superseded through navigation and appropriation by identifying numbers.[32] The high rise became the universal form of building. It could be adapted to hotels, offices, luxury condominiums, and public housing.[33]

Originally the clearing of space and the aggregation of dwellings into tall stacks were intended to allow the radiance of the enlightenment to suffuse the human condition. The goal was *la ville radieuse*.[34] But disorientation, mischief, and crime overtook the open spaces; neglect and decay invaded the apartment towers. In response, aggressiveness and individualism closed ranks. Authorities and developers gave up on public space and poor people, favoring instead the construction of high-rise buildings that were under the total control of private and monied interests. The public realm declined to a mere utility.[35]

Modernism has often been brutal, but it has never been totalitarian. It has inflicted terrible damage on nature and culture, but it has never obliterated them. Accordingly, architectural modernism has deeply wounded and disfigured our cities, but it has not annihilated them. It has destroyed New York's Pennsylvania Station. And while it has overshadowed Grand Central Station with the Pan Am building (as air traffic has overshadowed rail transport), it will never be allowed to level it.[36] Like intellectual modernism, architectural modernism is at last being questioned for the violence of its aggressiveness, the sterility of its universalism, and the desolation of its individualism.

In architecture we witness the most dramatic and public manifestation of postmodernism. In 1969, Vincent Scully concluded his history of American architecture with an anguished call to face up to the brutal force of modern architecture. His 1988 addendum begins thus: "An architectural revolution—some might call it a counterrevolution—has taken place since the previous page was written."[37] Aggression has yielded to preservation and accommodation; universalism has been replaced by eclecticism and pluralism; individualism has been rejected in favor of common and communal spaces.

Modernism has not been vanquished altogether. The institutional inertia of modern technology is daunting. Worse, the impatient simplicities of modernism remain powerful and attractive.[38] But as in the intellectual conversation, the iron grip of modernism has been broken forever in architecture. To be sure, postmodern builders are still struggling to achieve genuine splendor and contextual integrity.

The classical motifs, decorative paint, and sculptural articulation of postmodern highrises are usually draped over the same modern scaffolding that is at the core of a Mies van der Rohe skyscraper. Urban contextualism often provides but a more pleasant setting for a life that continues to oscillate between sullenness and hyperactivity. Precisely where attempts are made to build a place for public pleasures and practices, there is a feeling that these settings are vacuous or mindless at the center.[39] Still, one must be grateful for the gentler architectural climate. The task before us is to resolve postmodern ambiguity in favor of truly festive and well-grounded buildings.

THE
POSTMODERN
ECONOMY
The Decline of the
Modern Economy and
the Postmodern
Alternative

Postmodernism is most articulate in the intellectual conversation, most dramatic in architecture, and most pervasive in the economy. In the case of the economy, it is also most concealed. Its force is hidden by alternative labels like *postindustrial, electronic, service, information,* or *computer economy.* Yet there is a deep connection between recent economic developments and the postmodern movement that can be uncovered at different levels of evidence. At each level, however, this connection comes into focus most clearly when considered against the background of the modern project.

At the most obvious level, the postmodern character of the changes in the modern economy is evident in the observations of economists who are noting the erosion of realism, universalism, and individualism. To begin with realism, the modern domination of nature consisted in the exploitation of material resources—timber, ore, coal, oil—and in their transformation into material goods large and small, bridges and railroads, appliances and furniture. For Daniel Bell, extraction is the dominant economic activity of the preindustrial period, fabrication is that of the industrial period. Neither activity disappears in the postindustrial economy; both are overshadowed, however, by an activity Bell calls processing.[40] Accordingly, Eric Larson and his coauthors exhort us to recognize this historic change and look "beyond the era of materials."[41] For Bell, the rise and fall of aggressive realism is evident in the succession of the kind of corporation thought to be paradigmatic of the American economy, first U.S. Steel, then General Motors, and finally IBM.[42]

John Kenneth Galbraith depicts a similar passing of power from land by way of capital to expertise.[43] Land is, as we still say, *real* estate, the most tangible and enduring fundament of wealth. Or so it was until the Columbian discovery opened up seemingly endless resources of land and raised the value of what was needed to appropriate the land, namely, capital. Capital is less real than land; it is relatively mobile and, as financial capital, quite intangible. But the latter is always within hailing distance of the tangible assets to which it constitutes a claim; its power depends on being properly balanced with material goods. Expertise, however, is a source of power both intangible and nearly self-sufficient. It can generate extraordinary amounts of capital and goods without reliance on unusual material resources, as Japan has well demonstrated.

Cartesian universalism was realized economically in the giant corporations, a handful of which would dominate an entire economic sector. The corporation was intent on creating stability through universality, absorbing within itself, as far as feasible, production from raw materials to retailing, covering, if possible, the entire market, and all but taming the future through planning and capital resources. But the gigantic markets that once provided fertile fields for mass production are disappearing. Most recent economic growth has been among small specialized firms; the large corporations have shrunk or disintegrated. U.S. Steel has lost its very name and identity as a steel producer. GM's market share continues to decline. Even IBM has had to reduce its work force substantially. The remaining corporate giants are altering their very skeletons of methodical universality: their rigid hierarchical structures are giving way to flatter hierarchies and more flexible and decentralized forms of organization.[44]

Since individualism has led a divided and deceptive life in the modern economy, it is not a prominent object of postmodern apprehensions. But both its rugged and its commodious side have been reproached indirectly. Rugged individualism has provided the ideological cover for corporate self-determination. The nearly universal call for greater cooperation among firms and between industry and government is an implicit repudiation of ideological individualism. Commodious individualism gets chided obliquely for its excessive consumption when this country's trade imbalance and low savings rate are pilloried. The penchant for commodity comes in for scolding also when the growth of passive leisure leads an observer to muse "that America may have been evolving more into a post*industrious* society than a postindustrial one."[45]

Some of these symptoms of decline are specifically American and are often considered under the more inclusive heading of "America in Decline."[46] In this perspective, the weakening of the American economy may be a development within rather than of modernism. While the American economy is in relative decline, other modern economies, those of Japan and Germany for example, are thriving. Since for much of this century American business and industry were considered exemplary of the modern economy, the decline of the American economy may be exemplary of modernism, too.

At any rate, we must try to discover the deeper connections between the changes in the modern economy and the forces that first shaped it.[47] Evidently, the force of aggressive realism is slackening. It appears to weaken as the resistance of reality itself is receding. In a finite world, the subordination of material reality must be a self-limiting enterprise. At first nature and tradition constitute formidable opponents. At length they are overcome and reduced to pliable resources. As production and consumption expand at the centers of modern culture, natural resources and traditional practices are pushed to the margins. In the late twentieth century, the balance between centers and margins has become upset. The margins have grown thin and fragile; the centers have become bloated with consumption goods.

Resources like oil, ore, timber, and water are becoming scarce and more difficult to obtain. But this is the lesser of the perils that threaten the natural margins of modern technology. The more ominous danger is the fragility of the environment in its capacity to cushion and absorb the shocks and wastes of the modern project. A similar fraying can be observed in the traditional moral understandings that modernism has in part relied on for what cohesion and grace it has.[48]

Economic universalism, as we can see in retrospect, required for its growth and stability the very margins that have been attenuated by aggressive realism. Universalism needed the premodern cultural margins more than it did the untapped stores of land and raw materials. Obviously, modern mass production depended and thrived on readily accessible timber, ore, coal, oil, and agricultural land. But it relied even more on the lingering premodern austerity, the enormous receptacle for mass-produced goods. Likewise, it could count on the huge agricultural sector of the early modern period as a reservoir to provide labor for industrial growth and to absorb misery during industrial crises.

As the corporate economy became more expansive and productive, it exhausted its buffers and overcrowded its habitat. At every turn it now collides with obstacles of its own making: with oil fields that are running dry, with soil that is washing away, with rivers that can take no more effluents, with workers who have gained affluence and lost their docility, with markets that are saturated. Goods saturation, to be sure, is not a universal phenomenon. In developing countries, and even at the depressingly broad margins of our society, there is often a desperate and mortal lack of housing, food, drugs, chemicals, and implements. At the centers of the advanced industrial countries, however, goods saturation augurs the twilight of modernism. Even half a century ago, it must have seemed incredible that one day neither our space nor our time would be able to accommodate more cars, television sets, kitchen appliances, furniture, or sports equipment.[49] Yet, that day is coming into view. With it comes the exhaustion not only of our physical capacities but of the emotional hunger that fueled the immense productive efforts of the modern period.

Universal economic control, at war with itself, has to assume total control or recede into the background. Methodical totalitarianism is still a possibility, and for a while the multinational corporations were thought to be its vehicle. They appeared to be overpowering behemoths that could work their will on entire nations. But like any corporation, a multinational one operates in an environment that is partly beyond its control. It depends on the local availability of resources, transportation, communication, and skilled personnel; it is constrained by local taxes, environmental regulations, and labor laws. A multinational corporation can work in opposition to such conditions for a short time only and at its peril. It cannot hope to be the international successor of the modern hierarchical corporation, but it may well be a channel of the flexible global economy, where operations are quickly made to flow to the most favorable location on the globe.

The multinational corporation is global, but it is not universal, and certainly not totalitarian. Totalitarianism is a regime of all or nothing. Since it is a burdensome and costly system to install, its reward—certain and universally rising affluence—seems distant and precarious. Not that the calculus of utilities and probabilities compels the rejection of economic totalitarianism. Costs and expectations are always relative to one's situation and fortitude. But the latter are undergoing a ground-breaking shift toward openness and pluralism. This shift is one of the epochal marks of postmodernism.[50]

Rugged individualism, apart from the ideological service it was pressed into, is an authentic allusion to the vigor and self-reliance that inspired many American settlers to enormous exertions and accomplishments. Ruggedness in this sense was less often the father of the heroic feat than the mother of austere endurance. In either case it drew its strength from the necessity of hard and sometimes desperate circumstances, and from the joy of having for the first time ever a piece of land one could call one's own, or the mobility of a car, or a window on all the world's excitement through the screen of a television set.

As necessity and joy began to recede, so did ruggedness and application. A first indication that the country's collective discipline was beginning to relax was the American unwillingness in the 1960s to face up to the choice between military might in Vietnam and rising welfare at home. To opt for guns and butter both was to avoid present difficulty at the cost of worse difficulties to come. Next came the 1971 abandonment of the gold standard and fixed exchange rates to avoid the hard work and disciplined cooperation that would have been needed to bring the real American economy up to the level where it would match the grand assumption of American superiority that was enshrined in the exchange rates.

The oil shocks of the 1970s were also met by less than rugged responses. In the 1980s, finally, the weakening of this country's economic fiber became obvious to everyone. The United States still has the largest and most productive economy in the world, but its relative position is slipping. Productivity growth has declined by half since the 1960s. In the mid 1980s, foreign assets in this country began to outstrip American assets abroad, and imports began to exceed exports. These trends have continued to this day and are likely to do so as long as the U.S. savings rate remains so far below that of its competitors.[51]

There is, to be sure, a question of the accuracy of the figures on which this appraisal relies. Productivity, for example, can be measured in different ways, and the current measure may ignore substantial gains in the value of some of our products and services.[52] Ironically, the figures that betray our sullenness are so unreliable and unrealistic because we have been too sullen to undertake principled revisions in the conceptions of our data and to insure careful collection of the data as presently conceived.[53] Though one may quarrel with the quality and interpretation of the data and point to many a bright spot in the American economic picture, the cumulative force of our economic intuitions and experiences is depressing. In the common view, the negative impression we gain from figures and graphs agrees all too well with the growing presence of foreign economies in this country and the diminished sense of power and freedom one feels as an American in a foreign country.

Commodious individualism has failed to decline in step with its rugged kin. Borrowing from foreign economies has allowed us to raise consumption above what production would warrant. And so a twofold shadow now rests on consumption. Not only has the joy that once greeted ground-breaking consumption goods long left us, the enjoyment of consumption as the just reward of our labors has been undermined as well. Borrowed consumption is a furtive pleasure.

Yet in the sullen disarray of today's economy, we can discover the outline of an alternative and postmodern economy. For each of the modern principles a counterpossibility is emerging: information processing in place of aggressive realism, flexible specialization instead of methodical universalism, and informed cooperation rather than rugged individualism. As postmodernism has transformed the intellectual debate and architectural practice, so the formation of a postmodern economy constitutes a fundamental change. Considering the burdens of a desperately persistent modernism, one cannot but welcome such a change. Yet the crucial questions remain unresolved in the post-modern economy.

Information Information in the sense that concerns us
Processing here began as an extension of the human capacity to represent and recollect the things
and arrangements of daily life. More than ten thousand years ago, Near Eastern peoples used clay tokens to keep track of how many sheep were in which pasture, who had delivered how much wheat to the granary, and the like.[54] The inventions of writing and printing marked epochal advances in the growth of information and communication networks, enabling humans not only to render and remember more but to construct in the abstract machines, buildings, pieces of music, and social institutions that, once rendered concrete, exceeded in size, artfulness, and complexity anything human hands could have created immediately. Without the assistance of plans, maps, tables, lists, and ledgers, the conquest of the North American continent would have been much slower and feebler. Information constitutes both the skeleton and the lifeblood of powerful and far-flung organizations.

In extending human memory and conception, information renders the human mind more powerful. Until recently, the balance of power has remained heavily on the human side whether information was instrumental or final. Instrumental information consists of records and instructions that help us to produce and maintain things. Accounts assist us in keeping track of our possessions; engineering formulas aid us in constructing buildings. Final information consists of texts that may be enjoyed in their own right, for example, works of literature and musical scores. But both in the instrumental and the final case, human competence is indispensable to the value of information. One needs to be trained as an accountant to keep books and as an engineer to apply formulas. One needs to be literate to be capable of reading Shakespeare and trained to be able to play Bach.

The dominant position of human competence, however, sets a limit on the amount of information a person can usefully absorb. A hierarchical organization can square the amount of useful information once. But sooner or later perspicuity and mobility of formulas and data begin to congeal due to the foibles of the persons who are the depositories and vehicles of information in a large organization.

The growth of the communications network and the explosive development of computers in the second half of the century have made information not just necessary and useful for the modern economy but central and prominent. Computers owe their powerful position to the austere language they converse in, a language that has an alphabet of just two letters. The basically binary character of their language allows computers to transmit information through a simple change of voltage. To convey information by means of only two symbols is a tedious and expansive process. But the swiftness of electricity and its susceptibility to the most minute physical storage and manipulation more than compensate for the clumsiness and extendedness of the fundamental computer language. Thus computers can capture information with the precision of an alphabetic or digital language, can store vast amounts of information in billions of electronically defined spaces, and can manipulate and transmit information nearly at the speed of light. They process information.

At first computers were used chiefly as spacious and perspicuous containers of data. Electronic data management appeared just in time to save banks, insurance companies, the New York Stock Exchange, and government agencies from lapsing into sclerosis and finally paralysis, induced by an excess of data. Computers helped those institutions to contain their data and to let them flow.

The hopes that had been aroused by computers, of course, were grander. Computers not only were thought to be more powerful ledgers—containers of information—but electronic brains—users of information, agents of deliberation and direction. It was hoped that computers equipped with sensors and effectors would disburden humans of any and all dangerous, difficult, or tedious work. The goal was automation.

Robots, like an endless supply of clean energy, seemed an obviously imminent stage in the progress of technology. But the project of artificial intelligence and powerful intelligent devices bogged down in surprisingly or perhaps depressingly tedious details.[55] Yet technology advances flexibly and at many points. As long as computers were insufficiently sophisticated to close the loop from sensing a task by way of monitoring and evaluating it to directing and effecting it, there remained an opening into which humans were inserted to provide final control. What seems like making the best of an imperfect situation turned out to be an approach to work in its own right, as Shoshana Zuboff has pointed out.[56] The regrettable break in the loop of automation can be made into a window on the structure of an enterprise. What emerges in the window is not the physical appearance of the operation but a text that represents the devices and processes in a singularly penetrating way.

Of course, even in a nineteenth-century railroad company there were plans, maps, schedules, bills, and books that captured and pictured the past and present of the organization. Without such texts, as it were, the railroad would have been mired in collisions and confusions. Electronic texts, however, contain vastly more information. And while traditional texts provide coarse-grained snapshots, electronic texts can provide a densely structured moving image of a corporation, an image, moreover, that can be stopped, accelerated, magnified, reduced, and approached from different angles at will.

The electronic text of a business enterprise is so rich as to constitute a surrogate reality of the operation, and not merely a pale and imperfect copy of the real thing but a counterpart that exceeds its original in perspicuity and accessibility. Finally, the electronic text is even more than a brilliant image or model of reality; it is a superior reality. For to manipulate the electronic model is to manipulate the underlying reality. The electronic brain directs the mechanical body of the entire operation.

Almost any business enterprise can be electronically textualized and directed. Zuboff discusses paper mills, an insurance company, a bank, and a telephone system at length. James Rule and Paul Attewell in addition consider wholesale and retail trade, construction, and services.[57] To get a sense of the penetrating and illuminating power of computers, consider Dockside Grill, the name Rule and Attewell give to

> a computerized restaurant employing some 59 persons in a sub-
> urban location. Here, too, computerization serves to structure
> communications and work-flow. Waiters and waitresses take

orders as usual, then discreetly enter them at computer terminals throughout the establishment. Each order is printed out in the kitchen, and no other communication between waiters and waitresses and kitchen staff is normally permitted. No food is permitted to be prepared or leave the kitchen except as part of a computer-transmitted order. The machine displays to the waiter or waitress what had been ordered for each table, and the computerized order eventually is printed out in the form of a bill. The computer system both controls and streamlines the work of the dining room and kitchen staff. It makes it impossible, for example, for any food to be served that does not appear on the check. It makes it less likely that customers will be served anything other than what they ordered. And, according to the remarks both of dining room and kitchen staff, it obviates disputes between dining room and kitchen as to what really was ordered, disputes endemic in most restaurants.[58]

What strikes the layperson immediately is the applicability of computers to such a traditional and personal enterprise. One is hardly surprised to hear that wood chips on their way to becoming pulp and then paper are being watched, measured, manipulated, tested, and directed by computers. A restaurant seems like an organism, a community that would perish if computers were inserted into it. But information is being used, generated, and exchanged in such an operation, and the computer is introduced to secure, order, and refine it.

A computer does more, however. It renders aspects of the enterprise explicit and visible that a manager would sense intuitively but fallibly. Good managers know which waiters are efficient, what dishes are selling well on what days and time of day, and traditionally they have more to rely on than informal observation. There are checks, receipts, cash register tapes, bills, and more. But such information is scattered, clumsy, and at times unreliable. A computer furnishes a more complete, rational, and easily accessible picture of the restaurant operation.

Finally, the computer does even more than capture and picture an enterprise. It invades and transforms it. In the restaurant, the computer begins its invasion by replacing the social connective tissue that is made up of voices and shouts, of gestures and expressions, of rememberings and scribblings, of frustrations and of gratitudes. All this is superseded by computer links and memories. In time, the computerized system becomes the central intelligence of the enterprise—everything coheres and proceeds through the computer.

Computer networks not only assume the position of the central nervous system within a business but also integrate distant and relatively independent businesses into a single organism. In the clothing business, fiber producers, textile manufacturers, apparel makers, and retail stores used to offer each other their products on the basis of intuition and hope, matching one another's desires more or less, and incurring delays and losses all the while. A computer network infuses these several businesses with common and constant intelligence so that the joint enterprise produces precisely what is wanted, sells exactly what is produced, agrees jointly on what fibers will best serve which fabrics, and which fabrics are best for what style of clothing. In such ways the recalcitrance of distance, the obduracy of delays, and the obtrusiveness of unsold and useless merchandise are reduced.[59]

As Rule and Attewell note and Zuboff demonstrates emphatically, great effort is needed at first to discipline workers to a computer network, to prevent them from circumventing it by way of a person-to-person exchange, via traditional paper records, or through a walk to the vat of pulp that the computer claims is overflowing. Once such discipline is enforced, the computer system comes to be the central reality of a business; things and persons become its appendages. In a democracy, of course, no such development occurs without the consent or complicity of the people. But when the ruling pattern of the good life is taken to be commodious individualism, the expansion of the governing computer network agrees with everyone's desire to be disburdened of surly fellow workers, sloppy communication, and failing memories, to have more instantly the blessings of more numerous and refined commodities. In a restaurant, a computer accomplishes not only the disburdenment but also the enrichment. It eliminates the waste of dishes that were prepared in error and food that was bought in vain. A computer allows a restaurant to perform controlled experiments to find out what else customers would like to have, when they would like to have it, and how they respond to various improvements.

More generally, computerized information renders any and every material good less massive and inert. Computer-aided design allows an automotive engineer to vary and explore freely the thickness of materials or the configuration of components until an efficient solution is found. And computers or, at any rate, electronic devices are implanted in the very vehicle to see to our best comfort, security, and economy.[60]

Even in agriculture where we are dealing with soils, plants, and animals, computer information is beginning to displace the modern assault on the land through massive machinery and chemistry, an approach that did not come into its own until the modern period was coming to its end in the second half of this century. Today computerized information helps us to breed more productive and disease-resistant livestock and crops. It lets us monitor the weather, soil conditions, and the movement of pests, thus allowing us to time plantings auspiciously, use chemicals sparingly, and irrigate parsimoniously.[61] More generally again, computers allow us to construct a perspicuous model of the complex agricultural environment so that we can balance physical action and economic yield optimally. Well-aimed operations can afford to be less massive and intrusive.

Computerized information serves as the connective intelligence that organizes and rationalizes productive processes. It informs and refines the material products; it makes them "lite." Finally, it constitutes the very consumption goods that dominate late modern culture. At this stage, information does not merely organize and refine material reality but displaces it altogether. The ascent of information over matter, the movement "from things to thinking," has been hailed proudly by David Gelernter: "What iron, steel and reinforced concrete were in the late 19th and early 20th centuries, software is now: the preeminent medium for building new and visionary structures."[62]

Media technology converts these information structures into captivating sights and sounds. Information becomes final, an end in itself. It represents a breathtaking conflation of consumable richness and physical attenuation. Stereo components and a compact disc library, occupying ten cubic feet of space, generate hundreds of hours of music played by titanic orchestras and choirs. A big-screen television and video collection, taking up a few cubic feet more, display the vistas of continents and centuries of history. And all these sounds and sights are, or at any rate can and will be, of the most exquisite crispness and brilliance.

Flexible   Modern industry, since its birth in the late
Specialization   eighteenth century, confronted wide open
natural and cultural spaces for its products. Only mass production was able to fill them. Since the task was so obvious and massive, it made sense to dedicate a huge and specialized machinery to it. In this way millions of reapers, sewing machines, bicycles, automobiles, telephones, radios, refrigerators, and television sets were produced. After two hundred years of mass production, however, the natural and cultural spaces are filled up. Goods no longer have empty plains to flood. They now must compete for the nooks and crannies where obsolescence or wear provide openings for replacement. Consumers buy less copiously and more discriminatingly. The gigantic and rigidly specialized machinery of mass production is entirely too clumsy and prolix for this task; so is the large corporation that provided the economic structure for mass production.

There are, of course, huge areas around the globe that in the abstract represent open markets for durable consumer goods: Eastern Europe, the former Soviet Union, China, and the developing countries. But there is little these markets can offer in return. Raw materials have declined in importance. Ripping them brutally out of their environment to make them cheaper is no longer a matter of indifference to the First World, since in the industrially crowded postmodern era there is, from an environmental perspective, no longer any partitioning into a First, Second, and Third World. Technological progress and consumer goods will continue to spread into the rest of the world, but they will do so very slowly. This, at any rate, is what the late modern trajectory suggests. The postmodern crisis may be deep enough, however, to permit a more responsible solution to global inequity.

In any case, the paradigmatically postmodern economies of the advanced industrial countries represent a tightly structured and well-stocked environment. Economic activity is directed increasingly toward discovering small openings, niches and crevices that can be filled with highly sophisticated and specialized goods. Carol Fagan and

Catherine Engel, sisters who live in Montana's Bitterroot Valley, began making artful windsocks in 1985. Windsocks, both utilitarian and decorative, have long had their place in the economy. But the inventive sisters discovered an opening for "breeze-blown art," delicate and colorful creations that represent "puffins and poppies and wild prairie roses." They started in their parents' basement with hardly any ˜apital, assisted by their grandmother, mother, father, and nephew. Their real capital was education, skills, and resourcefulness. We are told that "Engel has a doctorate in zoology and was an accomplished artist in fabric media. Fagan had manufactured custom clothing and outdoor gear." Within five years they hired fifteen full-time employees, raised their production to 32,000 units a year for an international market, and increased their gross revenue by a factor of 250.[63]

The postmodern flavor of Wind Related, Fagan and Engel's firm, its flexibility and low capital cost as well as its luxuriance, come vividly into view when seen against another enterprise, located some fifty miles down the valley. Stone Container Corporation recently built a recycling plant there, a project that is postmodern in sparing the lives of thousands of trees yet modern in every other respect. It took several years of planning and one year of construction at a cost of sixteen million dollars to build a highly and inflexibly mechanized plant that turns 145,000 tons of old boxes annually into pulp for new boxes. It employs no more workers than Wind Related and does so at a capital cost of one million dollars per worker.[64]

Not all postmodern goods are as airy or as beautiful as the creatures of Wind Related. There are also machine tools made in southwestern Germany, fashionable fabrics produced in central Italy, steel rods and beams cast by minimills in the northeastern United States.[65] What all these firms have in common is their relatively small size, low capital cost, high level of skill, flexibility, and specialized production. They instantiate a new paradigm of production, flexible specialization as Michael Piore and Charles Sabel call it.[66] It does not constitute an altogether novel pattern of enterprise; rather, it is the successor of craft production. We commonly think of craft production as the late medieval artisanship that was doomed by the Industrial Revolution; but as Piore and Sabel show, it is entirely compatible with technological progress and in fact competed successfully with mass production wherever a highly differentiated market was to be supplied with quality goods produced by small expert firms that had the communal support of a family, municipality, or patron.[67]

In the late modern economy, a crowded market favors specialized goods, universal education can provide expertise, and families still provide communal support. This last element, however, is becoming less important. The mature and highly articulated economies of the advanced industrial nations offer an abundance of communication and transportation, allowing an entrepreneur to assemble from the general economic environment what previously had to be gathered and held together by a special community. Late modern affluence encourages risks and forgives failures that would have been forbidding in more austere circumstances. Increasingly, too, the paradigmatic competitors of flexible specialization, the giant corporations, are transforming themselves into a matrix for the new paradigm. They are rendering their structures less centralized and their facilities more versatile to provide a framework for flexible specialization.

Nowhere are flexibility and specialization more evident than in the service industry. Since it provides intangible goods, it needs no space for its offerings. It does require time, which it obtains by offering to do for clients what they used to do for themselves, or by offering to do in a sophisticated way what used to be done simply. Cautious citizens with cash on their hands used to go to a bank and open a savings account. Now banks offer you dozens of ways of protecting and profiting from your money. The possibilities are so complex that twelve million people in this country seek the services of financial planners, who inquire, worry, and decide for their clients.[68] There are professionals who will assume your worries about your dog's diet, the safety of your child vis-à-vis your house and vice versa, the mess of your files, and the frailty of your ego.[69]

The service industry appears to epitomize the new paradigm of flexible specialization; in fact, it is often thought to be definitive of the postmodern economy. It is a commonplace of contemporary economics that we are moving from a goods-producing to a service-oriented economy. Services have grown from a tenth of all employment four generations ago to three-quarters today.[70] But this simple and global trend conceals enormous diversity and complexity.[71] The Wall Street lawyers who earn two million dollars a year belong to the service industry; so do the janitors who clean their bathrooms and make a hundred times less. The service industry not only spans this depressing spectrum of social appreciation, it also extends along a dimension of greater or lesser proximity to goods production. A physician provides a pure if rarely simple service. But many lawyers and financiers support goods producers who would soon stop producing without the support of legal and financial services. More intricate still are the services that have their place within the producing firms and add to the safety, sophistication, and style of the products. Their contribution to the value of products is thought to be 75 to 85 percent on the average.[72]

The distinction between the goods-producing and the service industries obfuscates the concerns of social justice and the crucial patterns of the emerging postmodern economy. Flexible specialization is a better guide. It directs our attention to the ways the late modern economy is employing information and expertise to cope with a situation that is confined from without by the environment and is suffocating within from a surfeit of goods.

The rise of flexible specialization is not historically inevitable, nor is it totally triumphant or unambiguously beneficial. It might have already prevailed in the nineteenth century.[73] It could now be suppressed by a paradigm of total control. It will coexist indefinitely with the mass production of standard goods and with large corporations that take care of utilities. And it owes some of its flexibility to the misery of contingent labor. To the extent of its emergence, however, the new paradigm constitutes the signature of a new economic epoch. Yet even where it emerges clearly, it contains deep ambiguities that have yet to be resolved in the postmodern era.

Informed   When paper was the primary vehicle of in-
Cooperation formation, the latter was a precious com-
              modity. To make information find its way
to paper and assume an orderly arrangement there required many
people and much time. Once obtained and confined to a few copies,
information was a source of power. Hierarchical structures were required for the collection and empowered by the possession of informa-

tion. Computerized information, to the contrary, frequently collects by itself, incidental to what needs to be done anyway, like taking orders, ringing up sales, or using any device that can be monitored electronically. Computers can gather, order, and analyze all that information and make it available to anyone with a terminal. While paper favors a hierarchy of information and lines of authority, computers suggest a republic of information and a cooperative network.

Computerized information sponsors a new sort of cooperation and needs such cooperation in turn. Every kind of collective work will require cooperation. Rules are too brittle to undergird common enterprises. When a new collective effort is started, a factory, for example, rules at first are its only guide. Typically production begins haltingly and meagerly until a growing cooperative spirit, reflected in a rising learning curve, takes over. Any common concern can be brought to its knees when its members decide to set cooperation aside and do things strictly by the rules.

Computerized information is particularly in need of cooperation because it too is brittle and relatively incoherent. These debilities of information are sometimes highlighted by comparing them with the elasticity and coherence of knowledge.[74] Sophisticated software and automation project an organic and powerful presence that is sometimes thought to be equivalent to human presence of mind. But when such claims go beyond conjecture and theory, leading instead to a practice of entrusting difficult enterprises to automation attended by unknowledgeable humans, catastrophe is sure to follow.[75]

Conversely, when computerized information is embedded in a community of insightful and cooperative people, its transparency and power can be used to best advantage. In a conventional pulp mill, the chippers, cookers, boilers, pipes, and gauges constitute a physically rich and tangible environment. They provide an intelligible and familiar setting for action and cooperation. Vats are evidently full, the pulp has a definite look and feel, a valve is clearly open. When all such states and processes are monitored electronically and gathered as data on a screen, a more unified and perspicuous view of the operation is possible. But any such textualized representation is austere and ambiguous, too. Zuboff tells of an incident where an alarm went off in a pulp mill, indicating that a vat was overflowing. Other data said the vat was empty, yet the alarm could not be turned off. Operators and a manager gathered around the terminal. Suggestions, conjectures, and expeditions to various parts of the plant followed.[76] Such cooperation and conversation draw on many minds and experiences to generate a space of understanding and exploration, rich and definite enough to disclose the problem, a short circuit. One person would not be resourceful enough to generate it; a hierarchy of persons would have been too rigid and clumsy to construct it.

The paradigmatically postmodern firm is a small group of well-educated people, eager and alert to find market openings and to fill them quickly with high-quality goods or services. Informed cooperation is second nature here, a necessity of prosperity. It is otherwise in traditionally large and rigidly structured enterprises where information and computer technology are introduced ahead of the flexible and cooperative climate they require to prosper. There is a temptation to sustain hierarchies by artificially partitioning and rationing information, restricting communication among workers, and keeping their competence low.[77] One might think that to yield to the temptation is to invite a competitive disadvantage and eventually economic disaster.[78] But if this is true, it would not be because of iron necessity but because a general postmodern prospering of informed cooperation makes the economic climate inhospitable to rigid hierarchies. For a while, at any rate, the cover of rugged individualism will afford some protection for rigidity and domination.

In this country, lingering ideological individualism infects the relation of government and industry with particular virulence.[79] Limited cooperation has already been forced upon the unwilling American partners by the cooperative achievements of other countries. But the United States' high tolerance for crisis and disorder is retarding a positive and explicit embrace of collaboration. And at times, modernism once more and for the last time trips up postmodernism when critics of cooperation invite us to outline a system of coordination and then point out that any such system will be awkward, wasteful, and costly. So it will be, not because it is cooperative but because it is a system in the rigid and assertive modern sense. Postmodern cooperation, however, would be sustained not by a rigid structure but by shared information and flexible adaptation.[80]

4. HYPERMODERNISM

THE POWER
AND AMBIGUITY
OF POST-
MODERNISM

The intellectual, artistic, and economic developments of the past generation have led us beyond the broad and once fertile plains of modernism to a point where, looking back, we can see that we have risen irreversibly above the unworried aggressiveness, boundlessness, and unencumberedness of modernism. The latter now seems brash and heedless to us, if not downright arrogant and oppressive. The transition from modernism to postmodernism is reflected in many kindred shifts of sympathy: from the belief in a manifest destiny to respect for Native American wisdom, from white Anglo-Saxon protestant hegemony to ethnic pluralism, from male chauvinism to many kinds of feminism, from liberal democratic theory to communitarian reflections, from litigation to mediation, from heroic medical technology to the hospice movement, from industrialism to environmentalism, from hard to soft solutions.

There have been shifts from light to darkness as well: from enlightenment to dogmatism, from tolerance to ethnic strife, from liberalism to self-righteousness, from freedom to censorship. But in sum, the shifts to the good have prevailed. And nothing captures their character as well as the insight that the hard is brittle, oppressive, perilous, and finally weak; and that the soft is flexible, animating, stabilizing, and in the long run vigorous. This is the point that Amory Lovins urged prophetically when the emergence of the postmodern generation was approaching its midpoint. Lovins's avowed concern was energy policy. Yet his discussion unfolded broader patterns, a hard one that can only be called cataclysmic modernism, and a soft one that exhibited all the postmodern traits of adaptability, diversity, flexibility, sophistication, parsimony, community, restraint, and artisanship.[1]

Although too much is still done the hard way, this country as a whole is tending toward the soft and salutary path. Much of Lovins's advice has been followed. Hard solutions to the energy crisis have largely been avoided. Ironically, while applying ourselves to the sources of energy, a greater problem has overtaken us from behind: the ultimate and deleterious effects that energy consumption has on the composition of the atmosphere and the stability of the climate. Still, what we need is not a return to the hard path but a softer way of putting our planet in order.

Despite its beneficence, the transformative power of postmodernism is in doubt because it has failed to resolve the ambiguity of individualism. The latter term designates the human condition that has lost its premodern communal bonds. But we lack a unified and positive understanding of the person who would answer to the term. The individual was thought to be the beginning and end of the modern project, its author and beneficiary, but this coherence was an illusion.

The individual as author was in reality little more than an accomplice to a gigantic and systematic enterprise that, though resting on the consent of most people, was given a shape and momentum of its own. The individual as beneficiary, to be sure, was at first the heir to the benefits of more food, better shelter, and greater health. But mixed with those blessings from the beginning was the curse of distraction and disfranchisement. And though the benefits remained, the debilities grew disproportionately over time. The moderns have been reluctant to recognize that the ultimate irrelevance of rugged individualism and the ultimate debilitation of commodious individualism were the concomitants of the very character of the modern project. Its methodical universalism left no room for substantial individual vigor. Its aggressive realism so subdued and tamed reality that it no longer invigorated and ennobled individuals.

To be sure, this crucial fault in the modern project is marked officially and superficially by the line between production and consumption. But the line is taken to be obvious and unproblematical. The radicality of the postmodern crisis depends on whether that line is deeply considered and redrawn or not. So far postmodernism has failed to do this. The intellectual critique is essentially backward looking. It mourns the passing of the premodern communities and of the biblical and republican traditions; it regards individualism as the crucial destructive force. But this is to indict an anonymous perpetrator whose identity is known solely from the injuries that have been inflicted. The culprit's character, habits, residence, and very identity remain in the dark. In fact, the fatal damage to community has been done by a collective productive effort. The actual identity of the individual is that of the consumer. If individualism is not recognized and restrained in consumption, it will continue to flourish.

The economic critique of postmodernism has urged a turn away from the materially aggressive and methodically rigid character of the modern productive enterprise. It does distinguish implicitly between the rugged and commodious identities of individualism. While it rejects the former for its misleading and unproductive mischief, it finds the latter reprehensible to the extent that consumption of commodities lately has outrun the production of goods and services. To rein in consumption has been a standard ingredient of the medication prescribed by mainstream economists. But the implication invariably has been that the curtailment of consumption now is justified solely for the sake of greater consumption in the future.[2] The present criticism of commodity consumption thus turns out to be an unreserved affirmation of commodity consumption as such and hence of commodious individualism.

Postmodern criticism has yet to recognize that modernism is undergirded by a pattern whose chief feature is a division and coordination of counterparts, of production and consumption, of machinery and commodity, of labor and leisure, of the public and the private, of collectivism and individualism, of means and ends. The pattern is dimly foreshadowed in the difference between the Baconian and Cartesian design on the one hand and the Lockean design on the other. It was first elaborated in the Industrial Revolution and ever since has gained in power if not explicitness. It constitutes the template that modernity has taken as a guide in the transformation of reality.[3]

If we agree to call this distinctive approach to the reordering of the world modern technology, we should put the challenge to postmodernism by asking whether postmodernism will be more than technology by other means. It may seem surly to raise this question at a time when the dedication to technology has borne some of its sweetest fruit. One may well think of the recent developments in the former Soviet Union and Eastern Europe as the popular demand for the franchise in technology.

In a communist economy, the technological enterprise is arrogated, specified, and supervised by a cadre of the party; everyone else is reduced to a functionary within the central design. Party bosses alone are the stakeholders in the realm of technology. It turned out that when the pattern of technology fails to have undivided appropriation by everyone, it fails to prosper on the whole. One half of the pattern develops, to the extent that there is development, at the expense of the other—production more than consumption, machinery to the detriment of commodity, collectivism at the expense of individualism. If mature modern technology leads to sullenness and hyperactivity, stunted modern technology leads to worse—to grimness and suspicion, to suffering within and belligerence without. When the communist misunderstanding and mishandling of modern technology were pushed aside by deep and wide protests, the grim rigor of life within the communist countries was broken and the threat of global nuclear war lifted.

These secular changes for the better came to pass when people set out to claim their franchise in technology, taken as a comprehensive and distinctive form of life. They occurred, more precisely, when people reached for the peculiar amalgam of technology and liberal democracy that constitutes the common order of the advanced industrial countries. There is reason to believe that liberal democracy cannot be realized without technology.[4] Technology, it now appears, cannot prosper either without liberal democracy. At any rate, given its benign power, what reason could there now be to summon technology before a moral tribunal? Consider the prospects of the former Soviet Union, Eastern Europe, and, sooner or later, China. In the best case, they will recapitulate or resume the energetic appropriation of technology and enjoy the fresh appreciation of its fruits that the advanced industrial countries have passed through and left behind. In the long run, however, the recent converts will have to face the crisis of technology as well.

The end of the Cold War has aggravated the postmodern crisis, particularly in the United States. It has relaxed the tone and tension of our social integuments and ligaments. The public no longer snaps to attention and goes to work at the mention of communist aggression. Our habits and identity as the leader of the noncommunist world have been undermined. Though this, too, is a turn for the better, it makes a slide into sullenness or hyperactivity more likely. Thus the question we ask of postmodernism remains urgent: Will it be technology by other means or can it settle into a really other, more graceful kind of life?

HYPERREALITY Postmodernism must become, for better or
Instrumental worse, something other than modernism.
Hyperreality In its inchoate phase, it already exhibits
two distinct tendencies. The first is to re-
fine technology. Here postmodernism shares with modernism an un-reserved allegiance to technology, but it differs from modernism in giving technology a hyperfine and hypercomplex design. This ten-dency I call hypermodernism. The alternative tendency is to outgrow technology as a way of life and to put it in the service of reality, of the things that command our respect and grace our life. This I call postmodern realism.

Hypermodernism tends to produce hypertrophic versions of the three developments that are distinctive of the postmodern economy—information processing, flexible specialization, and informed coopera-tion. Of course, hypermodern tendencies are also visible in the intel-lectual debate and in architecture, but the former is not constructive enough and the latter is too solid to exhibit hypermodernism clearly. Once we recognize the hypermodern design in the economy, we can discover its spell among the intellectuals and architects, too.

Information processing attains its hypermodern exaggeration to the extent that it overcomes and displaces tangible reality. Even in its hypertrophic state, it continues to be patterned by technology and pre-serves the division of the realm of labor from the realm of leisure. The hypermodern modification of the former constitutes at first a painful and disorienting process. Workers who are accustomed to a tangible, audible, pungent, and spacious setting find it hard to gain entry, by way of monitor and keyboard, into the unreal world of computerized information. Zuboff has us listen to the anguished testimony of a pulp mill operator.

> "With computerization I am further away from my job than I have ever been before. I used to listen to the sounds the boiler makes and know just how it was running. I could look at the fire in the furnace and tell by its color how it was burning. I knew what kinds of adjustments were needed by the shades of color I saw. A lot of the men also said that there were smells that told you different things about how it was running. I feel uncomfortable being away from these sights and smells. Now I only have numbers to go by. I am scared of that boiler, and I feel that I should be closer to it in order to control it."[5]

But others, more richly endowed with what Zuboff calls intellective skills, begin to appropriate the world of information and learn to find coherence and power in it.[6] In fact, the new reality turns out to be superior to the old. It conforms more fully to the technological promise of liberation from the recalcitrance of things, the confusion of circumstances, and the foibles of human beings.[7]

It is an artificial reality, to be sure, but it is not a poor substitute. It surpasses traditional and natural reality in brilliance, richness, and pliability. Umberto Eco and Jean Baudrillard have aptly called it hyperreality.[8] In agreement with the pattern of technology we can distinguish its instrumental from its final version. We have seen how the former grows out of the postmodern response to the end of aggressive realism. Yet it is virulent beyond the exigencies of a finite and fragile environment. This is apparent in several ways.

Instrumental hyperreality, to start with, has ingested and digested the realm of abstraction that is the bequest of Cartesian universalism. To organize and control the assault on reality, it had become necessary to step back from the personal and immediate involvement in industry and commerce, to re-create and coordinate on paper and on a grand scale what forever would escape control were it attacked with bare hands. The results were the intricate and far-reaching legal and financial machineries that lent the modern economy coherence and resilience.

Being abstract to begin with, these machineries were predestined for absorption into instrumental hyperreality. Computers and communications first rendered the legal and financial world more perspicuous and pliable, then integrated and expanded it prodigiously. They did so locally by increasing the size and kinds of operations of law firms, accounting firms, and banks, and by enlarging the legal staff and financial departments of manufacturers, hospitals, utilities, and so forth. Hyperreality went global in space and time when the financial markets of the several continents were linked electronically, thereby constituting a twenty-four-hour financial trade that unrelentingly draws the legal and commercial sectors within its sleepless orbit.

To grasp the fascinating power of instrumental hyperreality, consider how slow and tedious the real construction of a factory is: land has to be acquired, zoning needs to be secured, plans are drawn up, bids are invited, the land is cleared. Now the recalcitrance of physical reality and human nature are only beginning to assert themselves. The water table turns out to be higher than expected. Local 45 of the Heavy Equipment Operators is shutting down the excavations because they are being done by nonunion labor. By now the corporation has covered a tenth of the ground it needs to cover before becoming the owner of a new manufacturing plant.

How swift and glorious in comparison is the acquisition of a corporation with dozens of plants by way of a legal and financial raid. Takeover specialists in a Wall Street law firm marshal hundreds of millions of dollars, dislocate thousands of workers, oust dozens of executives, enrich countless stockowners, beat out competitors, stay ahead of the Securities and Exchange Commission, all within a few heady and frenetic months. In the end, they bring media fame and tens of millions of dollars of fortune to themselves and their firm. It is clear why the legal and financial hyperreality, particularly in this country, has been drawing the nation's best talent.

Legal and financial hyperreality is an imaginary space of sundry doors and windows, among them telephones (both cellular and tethered), modems, computers (desktop, laptop, and palmtop), faxes, paging devices, and more. They and their information stores and links are still in the process of coalescence, a development that is advanced by a broad and powerful, if implicit, understanding of hyperreality.[9]

This intuition surfaces in a variety of explications. One that reveals the drive toward totality is the project of the scholar's workstation, where the screen together with the keyboard and manipulating devices is to open up a world that formerly was composed of real typewriters, easels, drafting tables, typesetting shops, laboratories, libraries (some of them continents away), conference rooms, and more. This new world, it has been said, "must be constrained only by a scholar's imagination not by artificially imposed technology barriers."[10]

While the workstation represents a culturally and dimensionally expansive hyperreal space, tentatively realized, flight simulation represents a definite three-dimensional hyperreality that is perfectly realized.[11] It is composed of a cockpit, mounted on a movable platform and enclosed by a projection surface on which a scene is displayed. Computers produce the sound, force, and motion of a rolling or flying Boeing 737, and supercomputers provide the image of Washington's National Airport, of an aircraft carrier, or of a landscape in Switzerland. The realism of flight simulation is astounding and verified by the fact that skills acquired in simulation carry over directly into the real world. And yet, being hyperreal, the simulator provides a superior setting for the tyro; constituting a perfectly realized hyperreal space, it prominently displays the characteristic features of hyperreality.

Flight simulation, unlike real flying, is pliable rather than recalcitrant. Say you want to practice landing. Reality would make you spend 95 percent of your time circling and taxiing. The simulator allows you to trim these margins and to make twenty times as many landings per hour.[12] Reality immerses you in the unrelenting flow of time; a simulator allows you to freeze a moment or replay an event. The real world of flying, moreover, is limited, compared with the richness of simulation. It would restrict you to, say, Washington's National Airport. In a simulator, a few button pushes will move you to Atlanta or wherever. While most real flights are thankfully uneventful if not boring, in a simulator you can have as much excitement, as many crises or catastrophes, as you like.[13] And finally, the real world is often confused, its contours, gradients, and obstacles being inconspicuous and hard to distinguish. A simulator can heighten and clarify them and provide a crisper and more perspicuous, that is, brilliant, reality.[14]

What is displayed here with preternatural clarity is struggling to the surface in the computer networks of the pulp mills, banks, telephone corporations, and drug manufacturers that Zuboff discusses.[15] It shows itself also and more partially in medicine. Medical imaging furnishes a hyperreal version of a patient that can be explored at will without actual physical intrusion. Medical expert systems promise, falsely I am sure, to provide a diagnostic space that will immediately and unfailingly disclose a person's ailments.[16] And a bit of supposedly therapeutic hyperreality has appeared on the windowless walls of hospital rooms, where computerized displays mimic an opening onto an idyllic scene that changes in programmed harmony with the course of the world outside.[17]

To prosper, instrumental hyperreality must retain the shape of a centaur. The refined part must remain attached to the crude part; information processing must be intimate with research, development, and manufacturing. There is concern among economists that American instrumental hyperreality will detach itself from its physical underparts and, like Icarus, take off on an irresponsible and treacherous course. Hyperreality floating free of a commitment to science and engineering turns into pseudoreality. It is by now an old saw that when faced with a problem Americans hire lawyers while Japanese hire engineers. Certainly, unless the United States regains a measure of affirmative if not aggressive realism, the physical structure that secures, supports, and promotes hyperreality will crumble, and so will hyperreality itself.

We can rest assured, however, that the common understanding of technology will limit the hypertrophic tendency of instrumental hyperreality. This type of hyperreality is still understood to be part of the machinery that will produce a commodious life. Commodity resting on whimsy is a contradiction within the framework of technology, where a life of disburdenment and enrichment needs to be guaranteed by arrangements and procedures patterned after scientific certainty and cogency. The technological temperament is sensitive to these requirements and can be relied on to support them, later rather than sooner in the United States, where tolerance for social and economic difficulties is high.

Final Hyperreality   Final hyperreality, unlike instrumental hyperreality, is not constrained by a reality principle. To render our intuitions about what is at stake more robust, consider a professional living in western Montana who has been offered an exciting and lucrative position in the Midwest. She is tempted to accept, but she will miss her daily runs through Hellgate Canyon along the Clark Fork River and her weekend forays into the Rattlesnake Wilderness. The employer counters with an offer of a paid membership in a health club where they have treadmills positioned in front of videoscreens so that the person who is running feels herself moving through the landscape that unfolds on the screen. The employer, in fact, offers to have videos shot of the candidate's favorite running trails.

Of course, what is being offered here is a poor substitute for the real thing. A sideward glance reveals not ninebark and mergansers, but fellow exercisers and a panoply of mechanical devices. The air is stagnant and stale, filled with humming and groaning noises. But imagine the scene elevated to hyperreal perfection: a panoramic, fine-grained, and vividly colorful screen; a running surface that rises and banks in coordination with the view that is being displayed; scented and temperature controlled blowers that simulate the air movement and fragrance according to the changes of shade, sunlight, and season; speakers that produce the sounds of rushing water, chirping birds, and whispering pines; monitors that adjust the velocity of sights, sounds, wind, and running surface according to the effort the runner expends. And assume that users of the perfect running simulator profess to be entirely captivated, exhilarated, and regenerated by it.

Before we pursue the moral of this story, let me use this example to formalize the three characteristic features of hyperreality exhibited so clearly in the final variant. Hyperreality is, first of all, brilliant. Brilliance has an inclusive and an exclusive aspect. It is to include all my senses entirely, not just my central vision, as the poor substitute does, but my peripheral vision, too. And not just my vision but also my hearing, smelling, sense of temperature, proprioception, and so on. A truly brilliant hyperreality will exclude all unwanted information, the visual or auditory cues, for example, that would betray the presence of the machinery beneath the hyperreal commodity. Technically, brilliance means absence of noise.

Second, hyperreality is rich. In the running simulator, the scenes of western Montana will have more wildlife, more thunder and lightning, more sunshine, deeper and drier snow. And it will offer our candidate not only runs in the Missoula valley but also around Diamond Head on Oahu and to St. Ottilien in the Black Forest. The ideal limit of hyperreality is encyclopedic completeness.

Finally, hyperreality is pliable, entirely subject to my desire and manipulation. Rocks, roots, rain, and bitter cold are banished from the hyperreal running trail. Drives to trailheads and waits for sunshine are obviated. The physical demands of any route are adjustable. Technically, pliability includes interactivity. I will use glamour as a collective term for brilliance, richness, and pliability.

The telos of hyperreal logic would be a perfectly glamorous simulator. Though a full execution of this project would founder on insuperable technical obstacles, the idea has immense power in regulating our imagination and has been prophesied by experts who should know better. William Gates, chairman of the board of Microsoft Corporation, says:

> "In 20 years the Information Age will be here, absolutely. The dream of having the world database at your fingertips will have become a reality. You'll even be able to call up a video show and place yourself in it."[18]

Tony Verna, president of Global Media and inventor of instant replay, has this prediction:

> "The viewer will be able to conquer space and time with the tube. Someday the director's and producer's jobs will end in the control room, and the viewer's job will begin. With laser vision, *you* are going to walk around in the scene. With sensavision *you'll* be able to feel the thrill of victory or the agony of defeat."[19]

Still, an unreachable goal can be a powerful motive force. The glamorous running simulator sketched above is technically possible and invites the question whether a person whose life is graced and sustained by runs through pristine forests and mountains might center her life in a glamorous Midwestern health spa as well as in the Rocky Mountain West. What is at stake when one centers life in final hyperreality?

Woody Allen has explored the question in his story "The Kugelmass Episode."

> Kugelmass, a Professor of Humanities at City College, was unhappily married for the second time. Daphne Kugelmass was an oaf. He also had two dull sons by his first wife, Flo, and was up to his neck in alimony and child support.

"I need a new woman," he says to his analyst.

> "I need to have an affair. I may not look the part, but I'm a man who needs romance. I need softness, I need flirtation. I'm not getting any younger, so before it's too late I want to make love in Venice, trade quips at '21,' and exchange coy glances over red wine and candlelight. You see what I'm saying?"[20]

It is not hard to see. But since the world had been so hard, austere, and troubled for Kugelmass, an affair would only aggravate these conditions. Consequently, Kugelmass turns to the pretechnological counterpart of electronics and computer technology, namely, magic. Allen describes for us how Persky, the magician and designer of a hyperreality generator, introduces Kugelmass, the first person to be transported into hyperreality, to the device.

> Persky went to the back room, and Kugelmass heard the sound of boxes and furniture being moved around. Persky reappeared, pushing before him a large object on squeaking roller-skate wheels. He moved some old handkerchiefs that were lying on its top and blew away a bit of dust. It was a cheap-looking Chinese cabinet, badly lacquered.

Kugelmass requests a hyperreal affair with Emma Bovary. Persky has Kugelmass enter the cabinet; he tosses in a paperback copy of Flaubert's novel and shuts the cabinet doors. Allen's account continues:

Persky rapped three times on the cabinet and then flung open the doors.

Kugelmass was gone. At the same moment, he appeared in the bedroom of Charles and Emma Bovary's house at Yonville. Before him was a beautiful woman, standing alone with her back turned to him as she folded some linen.[21]

And at least for a while, Kugelmass enjoys all the enchantments he had been hoping for.

Allen believes, however, that one cannot live peacefully both in a hyperreal and the real world. He deals with the issue again in his 1985 film *The Purple Rose of Cairo.* In both the story and the film, a crisis is precipitated when the hyperreal protagonists step out of the hyperreal into the real world, when Madame Bovary comes out of the novel and the dashing Tom Baxter out of the movie within the film. After brief euphoria, confusion ensues in both cases; the hyperreal protagonists return to their hyperreal homes, the real protagonists are left behind. Yet the latter cannot reconcile themselves to the real world. Kugelmass appears again at Persky's door "with a sheepish expression on his face."[22] Cecilia, the heroine of *The Purple Rose*, is last seen watching a Fred Astaire and Ginger Rogers movie.

Are these unhappy outcomes due to an intrinsic flaw of hyperreality or merely to the ineptness of the real protagonists in their appropriation of the hyperreal universe? Neither, one might reply. The fault may lie with Allen's misunderstanding of the hyperreal. His versions are not truly pliable. Had Persky provided Kugelmass with a perfectly glamorous hyperreality, Sidney would have had a pliable Emma, one that would not think of overstepping her hyperreal bounds.

But this is a misleading reply. Allen is moved by a deeper concern and claim. He proposes that the real and the hyperreal compete for our allegiance and fidelity. It appears that we finally cannot escape from the real into the hyperreal, nor can we settle for reality and escape the allure of hyperreality. How are we to judge Allen's proposition? There is no need to turn entirely to conjecture for an answer. Hyperreality has invaded our world in both dense and diffuse patterns. None of them, of course, is entirely glamorous. Yet glamour constitutes a helpful standard against which we can judge the extent of contemporary hyperreality.

Television is a dense and dominant presence in our leisure.[23] Ninety-six percent of all homes in the United States have color television; more than half of all households have at least two sets; nearly 70 percent have videocassette recorders; and more than half of our leisure time, as we have seen, is consumed by television.[24] If we think of television as the sum of programs that are broadcast or available on tape, it definitely fails the norm of glamour since it is not pliable, that is, interactive. Television also fails to be as brilliant as it might be. But there are intense efforts underway to make it more so, to provide better sound, to design larger and crisper screens within the local conventions of broadcasting, and to introduce the advanced technology of high-definition television.[25] The richness of television has increased tremendously during the last two decades with the growth of cable programs, the advent of dish antennas, and the expansion of the videocassette industry. Almost anyone these days can choose at any time from among hundreds of programs.

Video games constitute pliable or interactive hyperrealities, because a user can enter them and participate in shaping the course of events.[26] The modality of interaction as a rule is still limited to the manual, and to a narrow range of manual interaction at that. But here again endeavors are underway to admit more subtly tactile capacities of the hand and to engage the movement of the head and the feet as well. The goal, obviously, is to approximate on the side of pliability the active sensory completeness that would be the counterpart of receptive sensory completeness on the side of brilliance. In the higher reaches of technical perfection, of course, brilliance and pliability converge just as action and perception are largely one in the real world. The hyperreal life of video games is still coarse and jerky, but the brilliance of well-defined shapes and smooth action is rising from one consumer electronics show to the next, as is the richness of the number and kinds of games.

Electronic hyperreality is more diffuse in its hybrid versions, fusions of the real and the artificial. Computer networks represent such hybrid worlds. To be sure, they are normally installed with the sober intention of allowing users to communicate with one another and to provide access to information and services. Computer networks do serve those ends.[27] But people also use them to offer one another stylized versions of themselves for amorous or convivial entertainment.[28] So seen, a computer network is, within a narrow band, a totally interactive hyperreality. Communication is restricted to the narrow channel of a keyboard and a monitor, but within those bounds one can say and ask anything. In France's Teletel network of five million users there must also be a great variety of respondents. And it appears that the pliability and richness of this hyperreal realm more than make up for its utter lack of brilliance.

A more colorful hybrid of electronic reality and artifice surfaced in the presidential campaign of 1988. It featured, in the words of Maureen Dowd,

> Jack Tanner, a fictional presidential candidate who represents a higher reality to which the real candidates (who often seem fictitious) might aspire. His campaign slogan is "For Real" (occasionally misspelled "For Reel"), a thematic twist that implies that if a real candidate could only figure out how to run on a reality platform, it could really make a breakthrough. (Still with me?) As Sidney Blumenthal, the *Washington Post* reporter who serves as the show's political consultant, puts it: "We're aiming for sort of a suprareality."[29]

From there a continuum of the hyperreal extends toward the real, marked at various stages by dramatic recreations of news events, docudramas, and tendentious shooting and editing of the evening news.[30] This active blurring of the hyperreal boundaries is mirrored on the receiving side by the television viewers who confuse their real social distance from a star like Johnny Carson with the intimacy of his apparent presence in their homes and the real identity of an actress with the character of her roles.[31]

In music, the line between the real and hyperreal has been erased altogether. It would not occur to us, listening to a compact disc of Bach's *St. Matthew Passion*, that we were in the presence of anything less than veritable music. If it is hyperreal music, flawless and of supernatural brilliance and clarity, so much the better. Whether real music might be a matter of living persons gathering here and now with their tangible instruments, playing together as well as the grace of the hour has it, that question has long been dismissed.

Electronics has an elective affinity with hyperreality. It alone allows for the capacity of information and the swiftness of operation needed to conjure up a hyperreal universe. Newtonian physics and organic chemistry are slow and awkward in comparison, yet they, too, have served as vehicles for the diffusion of hyperreality. Chemistry has been employed to disburden us of the calories that are the unwelcome extension of the real foods we love. Cool Whip is hyperreal whipped cream, cheaper, more durable, and far less caloric than the real thing. Cool Whip does not need whipping and is free of cholesterol. Enormous efforts have been undertaken to provide us with fats and sugars devoid of calories. Nutritious foods, too, are engineered to be cheaper, more attractive and convenient, and more healthful.[32]

Once our eyes have been opened to hyperreality, its growth is visible in countless instances. Occasionally, it seems, hyperreality makes an example of a real thing and imposes its empire on a stronghold of reality that had seemed unassailable. Climbing, it would seem, is a response par excellence to the reality of a mountain, to its craggy, awesome, perilous face. And yet climbing walls have been reconstituted in fiberglass and moved indoors to provide ascents that are more athletic and variable and can be done more often.[33]

Like its instrumental complement, final hyperreality is still in the process of coalescence. Its electronic parts have yet to be adjusted and connected one to the other in their entirety. Here are mountains of grist for the mills of technology. The electronic, chemical, and physical components of hyperreality are being fitted to each other as well, and so the overlay of artificiality in late modern culture is getting denser and thicker every day. There are already fully integrated hyperreal islands of considerable size: Disney World presents a realm of glamour that even three or four days of exploration cannot exhaust.[34]

When we think of the reputation for cleanliness and wholesomeness that Disney World enjoys, and consider its annual intake of twenty-five million visitors, we may well become uncertain of our moral apprehensions regarding the reign of hyperreality.[35] The conventional norms of ethical theory have as much of a bearing on hyperreality as digestion has on sucrose polyester, a hyperreal fat.

> When the fatty acids were attached to sucrose instead of glycerol, as they would be in a molecule of fat, the resulting structure left no place for digestive enzymes to get a grip and begin breaking down the molecule. The result is that although olestra feels like fat in the mouth, acts like fat in cooking and will stain your tie if you drop a chicken leg fried in it on your chest, it is not in any sense a food.[36]

Nor does hyperreality as such appear to be, in any sense, a moral problem. Just as olestra is "digestively inert," hyperreality seems to be morally inert.[37] Of course, olestra can stain your tie, ruin a dish, or cause a chimney fire; hyperreality can abet pornography, encourage violence, or depress literacy.[38] But these are problems we find in reality, too. If we fix our moral concern on them, the line between the hyperreal and the real dissolves. But why insist on the distinction? Might it not be mere peevishness or sentimentality that make us hesitate to give hyperreality a fulsome embrace?

Consider once more the case with which we began. The professional woman, after a most stressful morning, is running in her favorite winter landscape. New snow is sparkling in the sun, yet the footing is perfect. Snow geese are vigorously rising from the river. Then it is quiet but for the scolding of the Steller's jays. A snowshoe hare up ahead is hopping along the trail. There, suddenly, is a crashing in the brush, a gigantic leaping and pouncing; a mountain lion has taken the hare and is loping back up the slope. Quiet once more settles on the valley. A herd of elk is browsing in the distance. The trail is rising. The runner is extending herself; she reaches the crest of the incline; another quarter mile and the trailhead comes into view.

Does it matter whether the setting of the run was a real or hyperreal landscape? The experience is the same, we are inclined to say, as long as the hyperreal landscape was perfectly glamorous. It would be the same experience since by stipulation the sensory inputs would be alike in either case. Yet underneath this truism there are profound differences.

Assume the woman is coming to the end of her run. She walks past the trailhead to the parking lot, gets in her car and drives down the snowy valley to her office. She is elated. People spend years in the mountains without ever seeing a lion. To see one at the height of a hunt is a rare blessing. And she feels blessed also to live in a region wide and wild enough to support mountain lions, and on a continent hospitable enough for geese to nest in the North and winter in the South. She revels in the severity of the early winter that has driven the snow geese south from Canada and the elk down from the high country. The snow must already be ten feet deep on the peaks and ridges. There will likely be a heavy runoff in the spring and strong river flows throughout the summer. This is where she wants to be.

Assume once more the woman is coming to the end of her run. The vista is dimming, the running surface is slowing down, the ceiling lights are coming on. She goes to the locker room, showers, changes, and steps into a muggy, hazy afternoon in the high-rise canyon of a big city. All that was true of the real run would now be false. The hyperreal run would have revealed nothing about her surroundings, would have bestowed no blessings on her, and would not have been an occasion for her to affirm her world.

Traditional theories of reality, what philosophers call ontologies, are as powerless to explicate the difference between the real and the hyperreal as are conventional theories of morality.[39] Hyperreality is ontologically inert, one might say. After all, hyperreality is physically as real as is reality. Unless the mean kinetic energy of the molecules of air in the hyperreal spa is really relatively low, there is no feeling of cold; unless the air is really compressed in the appropriately periodic ways, there is no sound of geese or jays. So with the light waves that convey visual information.

Yet there is a clear difference in the experiential force of hyperreality and reality. To grasp that force we must think of experience not as the sum total of sensory stimulation over a certain time but as an eminent encounter of a person with the world. The former notion of experience is indifferent to its context while the latter is oriented within the world. Hyperreality and reality may result in the same experience indifferently understood, but when the experience of hyperreality is oriented within its context, its force turns out to be disposable and discontinuous, that is, it turns out to have no real force at all. The hyperreal sunlit winter landscape is at the runner's disposal. She can call it up at any time, summer or winter, day or night. Once it is up, she can dispose of it as she likes—stop it, replay it, or exchange it for an autumnal setting in Hawaii. To be disposable, hyperreality must be experientially discontinuous with its context. If it were deeply rooted in its setting, it would take a laborious and protracted effort to deracinate and replace it. Reality encumbers and confines. Disposability and discontinuity are marks of hyperreal glamour, and glamour, in turn, is the sign of perfect commodity.

Commodities, glamorous ones especially, are alluring, but they are not sustaining.[40] A highly interactive hyperreality may provide you with fitness and coordination. Totally disburdening hyperrealities can keep emptiness at bay through ever more refined and aggressive stimulation. But since the realm of commodity is not yet total, we must sooner or later step out of it into the real world. It is typically a resentful and defeated return, resentful because reality compares so poorly with hyperreal glamour, defeated because reality with all its poverty inescapably asserts its claims on us, and, like Sidney Kugelmass, we have entirely failed the real Daphne while in the arms of the glamorous Emma.[41]

Reality is commanding and continuous in many ways. The mechanical reality of the technological machinery requires constant maintenance, replacement, and improvement. The oppressive reality of hunger, illness, or confinement unrelentingly scours and crushes people. Focal reality gathers and illuminates our world. There is in every case a symmetry between human life and its setting. A hyperreal setting fails to provide the tasks and blessings that call forth patience and vigor in people. Its insubstantial and disconnected glamour provokes disorientation and distraction, which are both precariously poised between sullen resentment and hyperactive exertion.[42]

To bring out the contrast between these symmetries is a task that is at once ontological, moral, aesthetic, theological, and political. It is ontological in raising the problem of what is real. It is moral in directing us to the very substance of human conduct. It is aesthetic as it involves us in the question of what human works are centrally enchanting and illuminating. It is theological because it leads us to the issues of grace and divinity. And it must become political and make us consider our responsibility for the common order. Either we see this task in all of its dimensions or we will miss it altogether.

Woody Allen has us consider the urgency and difficulty of the task. We cannot finally, he suggests, be citizens both of the hyperreal universe and of the real world. And if, like Kugelmass, we keep avoiding the issue and continue to succumb to the allure of hyperreality, a desolate fate awaits us. On his final journey into hyperreality, Kugelmass, instead of being transported into the charms of a novel, "had been projected into an old textbook, *Remedial Spanish*, and was running for his life over a barren, rocky terrain as the word *tener* ('to have')—a large and hairy irregular verb—raced after him on its spindly legs."[43] We have been running this way for a long time now and have left behind and lost forever, it seems sometimes, the world that once was "charged with the grandeur of God," celebrated by Hildegard of Bingen thus:

O most noble verdant growth,
Who is rooted in the sun,
And who shines in gleaming fairness
In the round
That no earthly skill will capture;
You are surrounded and embraced
By divine mysteries,
You glow like rubies in the dawn
And blaze like fire from the sun.[44]

HYPERACTIVITY   Flexible specialization provides a paradigm of industry that is superior in its setting and goal to gigantic corporations and mass production. Yet it is in danger of being subverted by a style of work that can only be called hyperactivity. To be sure, restless and limitless activity has always distinguished the modern movement. Observers have seen it take various shapes. In 1848, Marx and Engels singled out the bourgeoisie as the motive power of the modern project. With unequaled acuity they captured its endless and unceasing energy.

Constant revolutionizing of production, uninterrupted distur-
bance of all social conditions, everlasting uncertainty and agita-
tion distinguish the bourgeois epoch from all earlier ones. All
fixed, fast-frozen relations, with their train of ancient and venerable prejudices and opinions, are swept away, all new-formed
ones become antiquated before they can ossify. All that is solid
melts into air, all that is holy is profaned, and man is at last
compelled to face with sober senses his real conditions of life
and his relations with his kind.[45]

It would be hard to expose modern restlessness more starkly and
generally. Yet no generation since has felt truly forewarned. Each one
had to discover again the disorienting momentum of modernism and
distinguish it once more in its particular setting. Ernst Jünger re-
discovered it in 1930 when he looked back to the transformative force
of the First World War.[46] He thought of the war as the spark that
ignited the explosive combination of democracy and technology, setting off the conflagration he called total mobilization. War is its first
and clearest instance. In the twentieth century, it is no longer a limited affair, decided by the government and conducted by the military;
rather, it draws into its vortex the consent of all people and the efforts
of the entire economy. Total mobilization is not an ideological design
that is imposed forcibly on a people but the involvement of all endeavors and aspirations in a progressive movement. Jünger contemplated it
with fascination and finally with the ill-founded hope that it would
lead to a national renewal of Germany.[47]

Yet after every announcement of the technological conflagration,
much traditional and natural reality has remained to be consumed. As
more of it goes up in flames, people of energy and ambition are drawn
to stoking and fueling the fire. In the late 1950s, cardiologists became
concerned about the toll that this pyromaniacal exertion was beginning to take. The World Health Organization, contemplating coronary
heart disease a decade later, feared that it might "result in coming
years in the greatest epidemic mankind has faced."[48]

In 1959, Drs. Meyer Friedman and Ray Rosenman noticed a distinctive behavior pattern that preponderantly seemed to accompany

or induce coronary disease. It was a syndrome of intense and restless devotion to diverse and poorly defined goals.[49] The pattern, which Friedman and Rosenman called Type A, and its relation to heart trouble were confirmed by later research. The contours of Type A were more sharply drawn as a style of living

> characterized by *extremes of competitiveness, striving for achievement, aggressiveness (sometimes stringently repressed), haste, impatience, restlessness, hyperalertness, explosiveness of speech, tenseness of facial musculature and feelings of being under the pressure of time and under the challenge of responsibility.* Persons having this pattern are often so deeply committed to their vocation or profession that other aspects of their lives are relatively neglected.[50]

What we see emerging here are the outlines of hyperactivity, captured by the lens of coronary peril. The incidence of heart disease has since declined, yet hyperactivity is detectable today even without a clinical instrument. It shows up as the pressured life-style of "an overcommitted, 'frazzled' individual."[51] Indeed, without the real burden of disease and death, hyperactivity attains its archetypal shape as the style of life that totally corresponds to the condition of hyperreality.

To capture the fit of hyperactivity with hyperreality, one might think of the latter as a game and of the former as an addiction to that game. While reality is boundless in its difficulties, a game is always bounded by its board, its cards, or its playing surface and rules, thus secured against unforeseen aggravation. At the same time, a good game presents limitless possibilities and challenges within these protective boundaries. While the real world holds misery and grace, the hyperreal universe contains only news, challenges that demand one's reaction. And while in reality one may be defeated or redeemed, in hyperreality one can only win or lose. In the real world one may earn affection and gratitude; in the hyperreal framework there are only prizes and acclaim.

Hyperactivity at first seems contradictory—both overly narrow and poorly defined in its goals. But this contradiction is resolved when the hyperactive setting is seen as a game. Its boundaries and rules and the explicit conditions of success give it hyperreal precision. Yet from the standpoint of an uninitiated or recovering person, playing one more game, trying yet another strategy, scoring an additional victory, seem endless and pointless pursuits. Addicts think they know better. There is nothing so sweet as the ethereal and conclusive excitement of the game. Reality, in comparison, is dirty and interminably ambiguous. And it moves at the deliberate pace of daily, seasonal, and generational rhythms. The hyperreal game can be played at any time.

Consider the corporate advertising director who, when starting on her drive to work at 5:30 A.M., does not have to wait for the game to begin in her office. While in her car, she clicks on her cellular phone to check her voice mail and to call Europe. Take the partner at a leading international law firm who, when leaving his office and his brief at midnight, does not have to wait until the next day to have it typed but avails himself of the firm's twenty-four-hour word-processing crew.[52] And then there is the architect with his wife on the beach in Anguilla, supposedly on vacation, who remains in touch with his staff electronically.[53]

While a game is normally a domain within reality that is set off and sheltered from the world, hyperreality threatens to break through its bounds and inundate all there is. There are already hyperactive players for whom the hyperreal game has become total. Reality has been degraded to an adversary within the game, one who loses more often than not. There is no longer a distinction between playing and expanding the game. Whenever there is talk of a global economy, the notion of a total hyperreality is in the background. The image of global hyperreality reflects the notion of a game accurately. Being global, the hypermodern economy is limitless and, being hyperreal, it is cleansed of the hardness and darkness of reality. And so the emerging global economy affords a field of unequaled glamour, inviting ever more numerous and inventive moves: another brief, another memo, another proposal, another argument, another way to finance a project, defend a client, win a contract, defeat a competitor. This is what summoned Boyd Jefferies at 1:30 A.M., kept him until 7:00 P.M., and gave him the board on which to move banks, institutional investors, and takeover specialists into new combinations, to move quietly and then to strike, and to force others to play at his bidding.[54]

Since hyperreality has this affinity with a game, it tends to blur, for those who are fully attuned to it, the line between its instrumental and final halves, between labor and leisure. Of course, there is still, even for hyperactive professionals, a discernible realm of recreation and consumption. It is hyperactive in its own way, and it, too, was discovered and described early in its genesis. *The Harried Leisure Class* is the title of Staffan Linder's 1970 study describing the effects of the pressure of time on the leisure of affluent societies.[55] While the constraints on time have become more confining since 1970, other limits on leisure and consumption have been receding. Our impatience is indulged by the instant delivery of the most exotic goods; our particular tastes are obliged by customized products. Every one of our lazy or apprehensive inclinations is met by some service industry. Yet for all its florescence, the realm of leisure is secondary and finally unsatisfactory to hyperactivity. Leisure is playing at playing; it is not the game that counts.

Hyperactivity not only has its backside of leisure, it also has its underside of unloved labor and sullen leisure. Hyperactive work is treasured and hoarded, and it leaves a wasteland of mindless labor to the less driven and the less educated. This wasteland includes the lower reaches of the service industry—janitorial work, food preparation, waiting on tables—as well as the lower reaches of production, like assembly work, and of electronic data processing, such as data entry. What such work lacks in versatility and flexibility, it gains in controllability through electronic monitoring and recording. Externally induced stress in mindless labor is the unhappy counterpart of the intrinsic excitement of hyperactive work.

Since mindless work is uniquely exhausting and debilitating, its subjects are uniquely susceptible to disburdening and diverting hyperrealities. The latter in turn, alienating us most powerfully from the real world, make reentry into reality especially harsh and leave us sad and sullen. Becoming insensible to the radiance of reality, we become confined, as Dante has it, to an infernal and inarticulate condition.

"Sullen were we in the air made sweet by the Sun;
 in the glory of his shining our hearts poured
 a bitter smoke. Sullen were we begun;
sullen we lie forever in this ditch."
 This litany they gargle in their throats
 as if they sang, but lacked the words and pitch.[56]

HYPER- Due to its transparency and accessibility,
INTELLIGENCE computerized information invites informed
cooperation. Sharing knowledge and responsibility is the distinctively postmodern way of doing business, the successor to hoarding information and arranging work by way of subordination. Some authors have forecast a yet broader postmodern expansion of electronic communication that would enfold us in an encompassing communal structure and even unite us in a global village.[57] No reasonable person would oppose these warm and inclusive currents, yet they, too, are susceptible to hypermodern swelling and turbidity.

In any case, the network of computers and communications will become the characteristic infrastructure of the postmodern world.[58] It will consist of roughly four parts. The first is composed of the network's links: the wires, the fiber-optic cables, and the electromagnetic transmissions surface to surface or by way of a satellite. The second will consist of the sensors and monitors that connect the network to the world: cameras, reporters, and news services as well as more prosaic ones like polling devices, thermometers, and seismographs. The third part will be comprised of data bases including encyclopedic information, musical and theatrical performances, and records of all kinds. Finally, there will be information processors both for the purpose of keeping the network itself in order and to provide expert services of particular kinds.

Obviously some parts of the system are already in place; others are being added daily. The system as a whole has yet to pass through a period of intensive expansion and integration.[59] This emerging infrastructure can be analyzed differently.[60] But the present sketch allows us to comprehend the postmodern infrastructure through its likeness to human intelligence.

The information links are like the nerves that pervade and help to animate the human organism. The sensors and monitors are analogous to the human senses that put us in touch with the world. Data bases correspond to memory; the information processors perform the function of human reasoning and comprehension. Once the postmodern infrastructure is reasonably integrated it will greatly exceed human intelligence in reach, acuity, capacity, and precision. George Bugliarello, accordingly, has given this developing system the apt name of hyperintelligence.[61]

Why should the rise of hyperintelligence be cause for concern? There are, to begin with, problems of security and liberty.[62] Security is at risk because the software that constitutes the central intelligence of hyperintelligence is now so gigantic and complex that it exceeds all human ability to comprehend it in detail and to guarantee that a program is free of errors and will behave as intended. The design of ever more powerful programs becomes more and more protracted and precarious. The programs entrusted with regulating the traffic of communications in large systems have on occasion succumbed to chaos.[63] Security is threatened from another direction by programs that propagate themselves and destroy or displace information once they have been released into a network. Like the human brain, the hyperbrain is threatened by viruses with morbidity if not mortality.

Liberty appears to be imperiled by the construction and operation of hyperintelligence. If anything so immense and intricate like a hyperintelligent structure is to avoid the fate of the Tower of Babel, it can do so only through global design. And such an overarching order can come only from forceful decision and direction. But concentrated and decisive action inevitably excludes some alternatives and imposes one protocol rather than another. Hence it seems that hyperintelligence will have to incorporate universal structures of domination and exclusion. Once in operation, a centrally structured system seems to offer the possibility of total surveillance and control. Hyperintelligence contains so much information on each of us, and makes it available so quickly and easily, that we appear to be entirely at the mercy of a central intelligence.[64]

These dangers are obvious enough; yet there is reason to believe that technology as a way of dealing with the world has the resources to cope with such problems. Technology as a way of life has almost everyone's implicit assent. It is not on trial and required to sway a dubious jury with incontrovertible evidence of success. There will be time enough and space for second and third efforts, for improvisations and approximations. Human forbearance will fill the gaps left by technological imperfection. Accordingly, hyperintelligence, rather than conforming to a universal Cartesian design, will emerge piecemeal, with a great deal of untidiness and redundancy as well as robustness and resiliency. Security will prevail albeit at the price of some inelegance and inefficiency.

Liberty will prevail for similar reasons. Since hyperintelligence is an offspring of technology, it will be cared for by innumerable parents and will not depend on the severe hand of one patriarch. It will be cobbled together through numerous agreements and compromises by national and international parties. To be sure, advertisers and interest groups will use hyperintelligence to exert influence. But the extent of their power will be determined not by our helplessness but by our complicity. To be sure, one should not underestimate the technical challenges of global coordination and the legal tasks of protecting privacy. Neither should one forget that hyperintelligence will be a postmodern rather than a modern creature, nurtured with flexibility and cooperation rather than imposed as a universal hierarchy.

With security and liberty reasonably provided for, hyperintelligence seems destined to be the final instrument of fulfilling the promise of technology; it will enable us at last to "make ourselves the masters and possessors of nature" as Descartes has it.[65] That is the way it appears. But in reality, hyperintelligence, left to its hypertrophic tendencies, will lead to a severe diminution of human intelligence. Not that the hyperintelligent assault on the substance of human life will be an unprecedented and incomprehensible campaign. After all, pieces of hyperintelligence have been in place for a generation or more. What will be new are the intensification and coordination of these presently incipient and scattered effects.

Again we can get a sense of the gathering force of hyperintelligence by considering its analogy to human intelligence. While our native nervous system animates us and allows us to move with purpose and grace, the hyperintelligent system will be so extensive that it is everywhere already, obviating the need to move anywhere. It allows us to be in touch with everyone all the time. This ubiquity is often thought to favor universal connection and community, and this is surely so in a superficial sense. More deeply considered, however, the nervous system of hyperintelligence will disconnect us one from the other. If everyone is indifferently present regardless of where one is located on the globe, no one is commandingly present. Those who become present via a communication link have a diminished presence, since we can always make them vanish if their presence becomes burdensome. Moreover, we can protect ourselves from unwelcome persons altogether by using screening devices. Since I in turn am unwelcome to others, it will not be strictly true that everyone will be indifferently accessible to me. Yet that leaves a practical infinity of conversation partners.

The telephone network, of course, is an early version of hyperintelligent communication, and we know in what ways the telephone has led to disconnectedness. It has extinguished the seemingly austere communication via letters.[66] Yet this austerity was wealth in disguise. To write a letter one needed to sit down, collect one's thoughts and world, and commit them laboriously to paper. Such labor was a guide to concentration and responsibility. One was brought face to face with one's circumstances and forced to gather them into a succinct account. Correspondingly, readers of letters, faced with so spare and brief a document, had to concentrate on their correspondent and immerse themselves thoughtfully in the sender's world. A correspondence used to amount to a life's monument, carefully constructed and gratefully treasured.

Telephoning has also diminished the visits that bring us fully and really face to face with one another. To a visitor we perforce disclose our entire being such as it is here and now, in the sadness of our facial expression perhaps, the slump in our posture, the carelessness of our clothing, the disarray of our dwelling. But having so revealed ourselves, we can also hope for real consolation—a concerned look, a reassuring hand from someone who will clean up the table, wash the dishes, and fix the chair.

The extended network of hyperintelligence also disconnects us from the people we would meet incidentally at concerts, plays, and political gatherings. As it is, we are always and already linked to the music and entertainment we desire and to sources of political information. This immobile attachment to the web of communication works a twofold deprivation on our lives. It cuts us off from the pleasure of seeing people in the round and from the instruction of being seen and judged by them. It robs us of the social resonance that invigorates our concentration and acumen when we listen to music or watch a play.

This brings us to the effect that the ubiquitous senses of hyperintelligence have on the ways we appropriate our world. Again it seems that by having our hyperintelligent eyes and ears everywhere, we can attain world citizenship of unequaled scope and subtlety. But the world that is hyperintelligently spread out before us has lost its force and resistance. There is a symmetry between the depth of the world and our bodily incursion into it. In the real world, humans have a natural inclination to satisfy that symmetry daily through bodily intimacy with the world, walking about, feeling the weather, going on errands, handling things, and carrying burdens. Of course, humans have always been dependent for their wider world appropriation on indirect intelligence, on tales and gossip, and then on books and newspapers. But even when print mechanized and privatized the gathering of news, intelligence of the world retained a spatial and bodily reality. You have to get your paper, bring it in, sit down, unfold and hold it. The paper itself has its tangible extension and organization, its smell and its rustle.

The hyperintelligent sensorium, just because it is so acute and wide-ranging, presents the entire world to our eyes and ears and renders the remainder of the human body immobile and irrelevant. The symmetry of world and body falls to the level of a shallow if glamorous world and a hyperinformed yet disembodied person.

When we witness the moving decline of a person's memory, we come to realize that you are what you remember. What makes you a person in the world is the comprehension of the world, gathered and secured in your memory. Having collected and composed reality in our minds, we can meet the world at large on its own terms, as a microcosm standing over against the macrocosm. Literacy has extended our command over the world and rendered it more precarious. It made it possible to deposit knowledge rather than command it. But the literacy of writing and print again had an extended and spatial reality: it enforced a real competence of ordering and remembering the location of one's books, letters, notes, and papers.

Hyperintelligence disburdens us from having to remember either the immediacies of schedules, tasks, and appointments or the expanses of history, science, scholarship, literature, languages, or whatever else. A person might be stricken with amnesia while asleep. But as long as, on waking up, one remembers one's name and how to log on to hyperintelligence, one will be guided from appointment to appointment and furnished with summaries of what needs to be done. One can search out in minutes whatever information is needed and give it the appropriate form in a few minutes more.

Conversely, there are today people of sound minds who without their fledgling hyperintelligent support lapse into a helplessness not too far from amnesia. Nicholas Negroponte, who labors mightily at MIT's Media Lab to advance hyperintelligence, had entrusted vital data to his wrist watch and was worried about the finite life of his exterior memory. "Sure enough," Stewart Brand reports, "a few days later his watch battery ran down and the data evaporated; he was information-crippled for weeks."[67]

While truly hypermodern people will be crippled without their hyperintelligent information, traditional knowledge has become absurd with hyperintelligent information. If in the days of real scholarship you had a question about facial features in Renaissance paintings or about the origin of certain aphorisms in ancient Greek texts, you would consult scholars who had become intimate with art or literature through decades of travel and observation, or reading and study, and who had collected in their memory what was scattered in reality. Such people were venerable figures, revered for their diligence and intelligence.[68] Today, computerized images and hypertexts allow the novice to summon and select, within hours or days, answers more complete and accurate than the recollections of a scholarly lifetime.[69]

People who lose their memory lose their orientation. At first there are breaks and gaps in the command of their context; gradually the gaps of oblivion connect and surround them. Their past disintegrates into unrelated chunks of recollection. Their present shrinks to an ever smaller island of awareness and competence. At the limit, the person has become a thin wisp of humanity. Something less severe and yet troubling happens to people who surrender their substance to hyperintelligence. Plugged into the network of communications and computers, they seem to enjoy omniscience and omnipotence; severed from their network, they turn out to be insubstantial and disoriented. They no longer command their world as persons in their own right. Their conversation is without depth and wit; their attention is roving and vacuous; their sense of place is uncertain and fickle.

At the center of hyperintelligence is software that sustains the structure and facilitates the flow of information. It discharges an extraordinarily difficult and crucial task. But enthusiasts of artificial intelligence have been looking for it to take on yet more elevated responsibilities and to perform feats of judgment and ingenuity that will at length surpass human intelligence. These hopes have been blown up for more than a generation now. There is good reason to believe that an intelligence as widely ranging and commandingly present as that of a person is essentially and necessarily embodied in just the way it is now. Artificial reality most likely will remain confined to limited and instrumental tasks. The fear or hope that artificially intelligent creatures will make human beings obsolete is misplaced. Nor, accordingly, will hyperintelligence in either its peripheral or its central parts threaten humanity with extinction.[70]

Still, its power, if we indulge it, will be sufficient to attenuate our substance greatly. It has already begun to transform the social fabric, our commerce with reality, and the sense we have of our place in the world. At length it will lead to a disconnected, disembodied, and disoriented sort of life. The human substance will be diminished through a simultaneous diffusion and individuation of the person. Hyperintelligence allows us to diffuse our attention and action over ever more voluminous spaces. At the same time, we are shrinking to a source of instructions and finally to a point of arbitrary desires.

Hyperintelligence is neither a total nor an unavoidable overlay on the real world and human intelligence. It is obviously growing and thickening, suffocating reality and rendering humanity less mindful and intelligent. At an earlier time, as Thomas Aquinas shows, quoting his favorite philosopher Aristotle, human intelligence was intimacy with reality: "in the human soul there is something whereby it becomes everything and something whereby it makes everything. Hence we must emphasize that there is an active intelligence."[71]

5. POSTMODERN REALISM

MORAL DECISIONS AND MATERIAL CULTURE

In conducting our lives we make decisions large and small. In Western culture, decisions that particularly test or determine the worth of our lives are called moral. In the German tradition and increasingly in ours, "practical" is a synonym of "moral." The implication is that our crucial decisions concern our conduct, what we do rather than what we make. The segregation of doing from making, of morality from production, goes back to Aristotle and has been carried forward into the modern era by Immanuel Kant.[1] It has been a comforting tradition for philosophers and the public alike for it suggests that the modern developments that entirely upset and destroyed traditional production left morality intact, if not in its particulars, then, at any rate, in its general cast as the theory and practice of human conduct.

Some observers of modern culture do note disparities and tensions between contemporary doing and making, between ethics and technology. They complain that, while technology has advanced dramatically, our moral aptitude in dealing with it has not. But this complaint is as radically mistaken as the general divorce of doing from making. It fails to see that a technological accomplishment, the development and adoption of a technological device always and already constitutes a moral decision.

More precisely, what needs moral consideration in production is not so much the producing as the product. Insofar as production is a kind of doing, it is amenable to the application of conventional morality that has recently exfoliated on the branches of professional ethics, engineering ethics, business ethics, and risk assessment. What remains unexamined all the while is the power of products, of the material results of production, to shape our conduct profoundly. Any moral theory that thinks of the material setting of society as an essentially neutral stage is profoundly flawed and unhelpful; so, in fact, is most of modern and contemporary ethics.[2]

To lift the veil of moral inconsiderability from material culture we must consider more closely how people shape and follow the course of their lives.[3] We entrust our aspirations to daily and fundamental decisions. A daily decision is made on a particular day for that day. A fundamental decision is an action that looks ahead and binds us over many days to come. If my aspiration is to become conversant with Shakespeare's plays and I leave it to daily decisions, then I will decide every day, more or less, whether to read Shakespeare on that particular day and if so when, where, and what. If I act on my aspiration through a fundamental decision, I will enroll in "Shakespeare's Plays" at the local college, clear my calendar for the appropriate times, buy the books, pay the tuition, and make the implicit promise to my instructor and classmates that I will appear well prepared every Monday, Wednesday, and Friday at 8 A.M.

In this instance, to be sure, the daily and fundamental decisions are conventionally moral. They are deeds analyzable by the conventional ethics of promise making and keeping, of satisfaction maximization, of self-realization, of duties to self and others, and so on. Moreover, people have some sense of the relation between daily and fundamental decisions of the traditional sort. They sense that daily decisions must be consonant with fundamental ones and that, should there be dissonance, the daily decisions will wither and die along with the aspiration assigned to them. On New Year's Eve, however, this truth too often becomes the victim of drink and sentimentality.

Even more frequent than the failure to make a suitable fundamental decision is the making of a fundamental moral decision without responsible insight. These are typically decisions about the shaping of our material environment. The father who in the early fifties brought home a television set to surprise and gladden his family likely persuaded himself that this device would be an addition and an enrichment to the life of his family. They would be able to see a play by Shakespeare, watch the news, follow a ball game, and otherwise life would proceed as always, albeit more richly informed.

Gary Larsen has pictured this father and his family "in the days before television." Dad is sitting on the couch, son and daughter lying on the floor, the dog between them, all four staring at the same blank wall.[4] Once the situation that was tacitly assumed is rendered explicit, it becomes a cartoon and reveals the absurdity of the assumption that life has empty slots that can be filled without needing to rearrange the order of life. Life is always and already full; it is a total fabric. It may contain empty spaces for inconsequential additions. But if anything is added to life that takes time, the web of life is torn and rewoven; a hole is made by the new device. Saving and taking time come to the same thing here. A timesaving device creates a hole in traditional practices no less than does a device that devours time.

Once a television set is in the house, the daily decision whether to read a book, or write a letter, or play a game, or tell stories, or go for a walk, or sit down to dinner, or watch television no longer really ranges over seven possibilities. The presence of television has compressed all alternatives to one whose subalternatives are contained in the question: What are we going to watch tonight?

Or consider the mother who has been told earnestly and often by her teenage daughter that a car of her own would disburden the mother from having to ferry her daughter from school to flute lessons on Wednesday afternoons and from home to the track meet on Saturday mornings. And with a car of her own she could hold a job on weekends and take up cross-country skiing in the winter. If the mother relents and gets her daughter the car, the question for this mobile teenager is no longer whether to stay home on weekends to practice her flute or have her friends over but only where to drive, to what safely distant and irresistibly exciting beach, or disco, or drive-in, or mall, or whatever.

The moral fabric of family life is typically patterned not so much by practices as by acquisitions, by material decisions, as I will call them, rather than by practical decisions. Of course, parents do not make their fundamental material decisions in a vacuum. The purchase of a television set becomes an apparently irresistible proposition when sets are relatively cheap and programs attractive. A car for a teenager seemingly becomes a necessity when the social fabric of a neighborhood has become too thin to provide lively places for youngsters within it and when public institutions have been so scattered and public transportation so emaciated that without a car a vigorous life demands heroic and exhausting exertion of parents and offspring.

Evidently, the individuals' fundamental material decisions are embedded in collective fundamental decisions that pattern the tangible social setting. The individuals' daily and practical decisions are to their fundamental and material decisions as the latter are to collective material decisions. In each instance, the latter powerfully preform the former. Our collective fundamental and material decisions, then, are of the greatest moral significance. How do they come to be made? Most theorists would fail to see or will even deny that they are being made at all. The conservatives resort, as we have seen, to rugged individualism as an escape from collective responsibility. Liberals fervently embrace this collective responsibility, but they are so preoccupied with its practical dimension that they are blind to the material one. The liberals' preoccupation is surely an honorable one, focused as it is on civil rights and criminal procedure. Their concern is of long standing in this country and eminently reflected in the Constitution.

Yet even at the very outset of the changes that were to reshape the material conditions of life from the ground up, the Founding Fathers recognized that the Constitution had to contain a narrow opening at least for the exercise of collective power and responsibility in the direction of material change. The interstate commerce clause was that opening, and the exigencies of technological progress meanwhile have excavated it into a broad channel of federal action.

There is some truth, to be sure, in the general sentiment that the technological transformation of the world has not and could not have been accomplished chiefly through governmental design. Communism has been the experiment on that hypothesis, and the results are now in. Technology has been a broadly embraced project in the successful industrial countries; everyone has been implicated in it. So, too, has government. The transcontinental building of railroads could not have proceeded had the federal government not provided for charters of incorporation, granted vast tracts of land, secured easements, and limited liability.[5] In fact, the railroad industry would have suffered less corruption and fewer cataclysms if the federal government had acted more energetically and constructively. In the early and middle parts of this century, government at various levels abetted the brutal reshaping of the urban order through the exercise of eminent domain, incentive zoning, and massive infusions of money.[6] In 1956, the federal government began the construction of the interstate highway system that a generation later comprised forty-four thousand miles.[7]

Both urban renewal and the interstate project were promoted politically through specious and inaccurate reasoning. Health, safety, efficiency, and economic vitality were invoked for justification. The profound, often violent, and deadening effects of these policies were never considered concretely and in detail.[8] This indirection illustrates the common uneasiness with the collective shaping of material culture. When in the late seventies and early eighties a feeble attempt at an explicit assumption of responsibility was made under the heading of industrial policy, its partisan proponents were soundly defeated by public opinion.[9] Yet the conservative government that hoisted the flag of rugged individualism once more in the eighties found itself implicated in something like an industrial policy. It proposed to spend 4.4 billion dollars on a superconducting supercollider, developed a superconductive initiative that was to relax antitrust laws to promote industrial collaboration, and announced its support of Sematech to assist the semiconductor industry. It unveiled a high-performance computing strategy, promising 1.7 billion dollars in support over five years, and it promoted numerous smaller projects to advance computer-integrated robotics and computer-aided design.[10] More recently there have been legislative efforts to support domestic research and development of advanced memory chips and high-definition television and to promote an interstate fiber-optic communications system.

Conservatives and liberals converge on the same position regarding the material culture. Both parties want to entrust it to the sovereignty of the consumer. The conservatives like the consumers' setting, the free market, because of its reliability as a bulwark of conservative privileges while the liberals see in the consumers' discretion and range of choices the warrant of a value-neutral public sphere. But to extol the consumer is to deny the citizen. When consumers begin to act, the fundamental decisions have already been made. Consumers are in a politically and morally weak position. They are politically weak because the signals that they can send to the authorities about the common order are for the most part ambiguous. Does the purchase of an article signal approval, thoughtlessness, or lack of a better alternative? Does the refusal to buy show dissatisfaction with the style of the article, its safety, durability, or its very existence? Matters are more confusing still since any action is understandable only in the context of rival actions contemplated and foregone.

A consumer is in a morally weak position in the same way that anyone is relatively helpless in the exercise of daily decisions. Daily decisions are preformed by fundamental decisions. The fundamental and material decisions that have shaped the technological society leave little leeway to the daily decisions of the consumer. My decisions, day after day, to buy my produce at the farmers' market will come to little, and eventually to nothing, if the farmers' market is in a grimy area at the other end of town and has little to offer while the supermarket is on my way home and has everything my heart desires.

Even if the government were not implicated in the construction of the tangible order of things, it would constitute the obvious instrument for a free people to assert its will if it is dissatisfied with the shape the physical environment is assuming. The failure of people and parties to take clear and vigorous responsibility for the order of things indicates the absence of any profound disagreement with the tangible character of contemporary life. Yet it would be hasty to infer general approval from the lack of patent discontent. Between wholehearted approval and strenuous rejection lies something like implication in a course of events, the half-knowing and half-hearted going along and even pushing ahead with a certain sort of development.

Implication in this sense, I suggest, characterizes the common attitude toward technology and toward its most recent hypermodern possibility. Once again we are being implicated as citizens who approve of public measures to promote hyperreality, hyperactivity, and hyperintelligence, and as consumers who yield to the glamour, fever, and ethereal charm of the new condition. Such implication, however, is fraught with misgivings and sorrows, and in these sentiments a genuine alternative quietly asserts itself. If it is to be vital, the alternative must be postmodern. Anyone who wants to encourage it therefore must avoid those attempts at support that are aggressive, universal, or individualistic. What we need in particular are not more effective procedures for the general will to have its way, but a real conversation. We must talk in the public forum about the things that finally matter and about common measures that will give these things a secure and prominent place in our midst.

FOCAL REALISM　　How can we hope to contain the distracting and enfeebling force of hypermodernism? Since we are implicated collectively in the fundamental measures that presently are establishing a hypermodern culture, only clearsighted and public action can reverse the prevailing tendency. But what actions specifically? Should the government embargo funding for research and development in electronics, computers, communications, and media technology? Should legal limits be imposed on the length of everyone's workweek? Should the construction of a nationwide fiber-optic system be prohibited? Even if such measures were enforceable, they would be stifling and odious. The ingenuity of modern technology, not to mention that of science, represents one of the great creative achievements of humanity. It would impoverish the human spirit severely if the regular stream of scientific research and technological innovation were to be dammed. To be sure, there are landmarks of science and technology policy that require us to say yes or no to a particular project through legislative action—no to supersonic passenger planes, yes to the superconducting supercollider. And the countless decisions the government makes about the flow of science and technology should obviously channel it toward the salutary and substantial, away from the dubious and frivolous.

At any rate, hypermodernism in general can be met not through embargoes and prohibitions but through a genuine alternative. In a finite world, devotion to one thing will curb indulgence in another. Devotion to the proper alternative I propose to call postmodern realism. It is an orientation that accepts the lessons of the postmodernist critique and resolves the ambiguities of the postmodern condition in an attitude of patient vigor for a common order centered on communal celebrations. What can invigorate the attitude and provide a center for celebration is reality.

How can reality be central to any postmodern orientation when the first target of postmodern criticism has been realism? It is true that both aggressive realism and philosophical or metaphysical realism have been stripped of credibility and authority by their postmodern critics. What has really fallen victim to the critique, however, is not reality but the aggressive and methodical assault on it. Such an attack either destroys or misses reality, and under the sway of modern realism, reality at length vanishes or becomes invisible.

Postmodern criticism gets arrested prematurely, however, when, having considered critically the modern arrogation of reality, it accepts naively the legacy of that arrogance, namely, the disappearance of reality. Worse, postmodern criticism gets caught in dogmatism when it restricts the postmodern conversation to humanity and dismisses without further thought the possibility of eloquent things. The postmodern theorists have discredited ethnocentrism and logocentrism so zealously that they have failed to see their own anthropocentrism. Why reject a priori the very possibility that things may speak to us in their own right?

It is only a possibility. To secure reality with necessity was the impossible program of modern philosophy. What one may truly hope for is that reality actually comes to be present. But how could it do so on the pages of a book? The only reality author and reader can be sure of are traces of ink on the page. These marks, no matter how real, would be forever silent were they not embedded in a communal context wherein they invite and instruct the reader to recall or call forth a certain reality. A text by itself is helpless; to require help is its virtue. The requirements for its vitality are the existence of a literate community and the presence of an eloquent reality.[11] These certainly should be the conditions of life. When they are circumvented and life is conjured up without them, hyperreality is the result. Instructions to call up reality can be more or less particular and pregnant. Here I want to provide a general and schematic survey of the landscape of reality and point to the focal points within it. I will present reality on its particular terms and by its proper names when we come to communal celebration.

Though there is just one reality, it can be surveyed from many points. Physics invites us to view it from close up and far away. It discloses the lawful microstructure of reality, that of atoms, atomic particles, and perhaps far smaller parts such as strings; it reveals the macrostructures of solar systems, galaxies, and clusters of galaxies. While universal lawfulness may be thought of as the distinctive feature of modern physics, we can think of postmodern physics as distinguished by the realization that the presently manifold lawfulness of the very small and very large has its origin and comprehension in the unique story of a particular thing—the origin of the cosmos from the big bang. The physical account of the world has decisive boundary force. It sets definitive limits on orientation and explanation. Any credible view of reality must be consistent with the cosmological and microphysical conditions so far uncovered by physics. But the reality that finally matters lies between the physical microscale and macroscale. It must be granted its proper scale like a painting that would vanish as such if viewed through a microscope or from a satellite.[12]

This middle region of physical reality is divided today by the line between the real and the hyperreal. On the one side are things of commanding presence, continuous with the world; on the other, disposable and discontinuous experiences. This dividing line is in one respect coincident with the technological division between machinery and commodity. Final hyperreality is a commodity; it is not disposable and discontinuous simply but only on the basis of a sophisticated machinery. The machinery is neither disposable nor discontinuous. It demands ingenuity and attention; it needs to be secured in space and connected to energy sources if it is to work. Instrumental hyperreality straddles and obscures this division while it continues to depend on it.

We may call the reality of the machinery mechanical in a broad sense that includes the electrical and chemical. Though it is real enough, it is also silent. It works, after all, in the service of the commodity that has sole claim to prominence and glamour. It is a sign of technological imperfection when mechanical reality becomes or still is noisy and obtrusive. The silence of the perfect technological machinery subdues not only the machinery proper but also its ultimate margins, what we now call resources. Rivers are muted when they are dammed; prairies are silenced when they are stripped for coal; mountains become torpid when they are logged. Technology is far from perfectly powerful, however, and its marginal reality is in many ways obstructive and obstreperous. It refuses to absorb our wastes and fails to yield enough water and oil. And though medical technology has made enormous advances against illness and death, it has left uncontrollable margins of morbidity and mortality.

On the other side of hyperreality and its supporting mechanical and marginal reality lies eloquent reality. It speaks in its own right and in many voices. It speaks in asides and in sermons. At times it troubles and threatens, at other times it consoles and inspires. An approximate and familiar appellation for "eloquent" is "natural" or "traditional." Premodern reality was entirely natural and traditional, and typically it was locally bounded, cosmically centered, and divinely constituted. Postmodern reality is natural and traditional only in places where hyperreality and its mechanical supports have left openings. On closer inspection, the line between hyperreality and eloquent reality turns out to be heavily reticulated. Hyperreality is like a thickening network that overlies and obscures the underlying natural and traditional reality. At the limit, the hyperreal overlay will have choked off the underlying reality and reduced it entirely to a mechanical and marginal condition.

Still, this is not the postmodern condition. There are yet generous openings for eloquent reality. In fact, it is hard to imagine how there could ever be more than openings. Technological aids to human life have become indispensable, and no one should wish them away. The indispensability of some sort of technological machinery is no misfortune. It is compatible with eloquent reality, as are many of the technological commodities. Eloquent reality would find itself in mortal danger only if the technological machinery were to luxuriate in an unchecked profusion of hyperreal commodities.

The counterforce to this tendency is eloquent reality itself, particularly where it emerges to gather our thoughts and ways and to illuminate the postmodern condition. I call such reality focal. The term "focal reality" in an essay such as this is simply a placeholder for the encounters each of us has with things that of themselves have engaged mind and body and centered our lives. Commanding presence, continuity with the world, and centering power are signs of focal things. They are not warrants, however. Focal things warrant themselves. To present them is never more than to recall them.

My concern right now is merely to recollect them from afar so that they become visible in their underlying coherence. On this continent the wilderness has the clearest voice among eloquent things. In its place it possesses an unbroken continuity with the land. If it is not as it has always been, it certainly is the closest descendant of the primeval world. And so the voice of the wilderness has a powerfully commanding resonance, too, because it shows no traces of human intonation. It speaks to us naturally. To be sure, it speaks out of the past into a present that is largely technological. No one who ventures into the wilderness can ever entirely forget that technology envelops the wilderness and could at any time strangle it. But to a truly post-modern sensibility, the lack of unassailable hardness on the part of the wilderness is not a sign of weakness.

Outside of the wilderness, everything shows the imprint of a human hand. One might think that the mark of human creativity is like the brand on a horse that identifies it as a human possession and denies it any possibility to speak on its own behalf. In fact, a domestic horse is not just a human possession but a human product, the result of millennia of breeding. But were the status of focal things to be determined by universal criteria, we would relapse into modernism. Let things speak for themselves. Horses do so with peerless power and grace.

There is a whole range of domesticated nature full of eloquent things. Though their focal reality cannot be adjudicated generally, we know from experience that plants and animals can become weak and faint. They can lose all focal significance when they are deracinated entirely from their ancestral ground and degraded to tool or toy, like a hydroponic tomato plant under growing lights or a debarked poodle forever confined to a condominium.

In the crafts, humanity enters into an intimate and active engagement with nature. Natural materials—stone, clay, metal, wood, hides, fibers—are taken up and transformed by the artisan. Nature does not disappear in the crafted piece; it is revealed and celebrated in new forms, strips of red cedar in a canoe, strips of Tonkin bamboo in a fishing rod.[13] These things bespeak their natural origin and anticipate the natural setting of streams and lakes. Others, such as violins or bowls, point to musical or domestic settings. Crafts are as deeply traditional as they are natural. They embody the experiences artisans have had with the materials of nature and the purposes and circumstances of their communities.

A violin by Stradivari goes back to the late seventeenth or early eighteenth century and stands itself at the endpoint of a long chain of string instruments. It tells of the baroque music it was designed for and of the musical traditions it has served since. One can find a Stradivarius in a glass case at the Metropolitan Museum of Art in New York City or in the embrace of Yo-Yo Ma. Museums are designated as protective precincts for the most eloquent things humans have created, works of art. But there is a thin line between protection and imprisonment, between exhibition and evisceration or even desecration. There is an order of reverence among institutions. At the lower end is the museum of anthropology, where sacred articles are displayed as curious or scholarly materials. At the mid level is the art gallery, where such objects are honored as works of art. The concert hall or sanctuary stands at the apex, where such a thing has its focal place in a sacred practice.

Surely a Stradivarius is placed more appropriately in the playing of a cellist or violinist than in an exhibition of the Metropolitan Museum. Things can be focal only in the care of human practices—a wilderness in hiking; a horse in grooming, training, and riding; a rod in fishing. Focal reality is alive in the symmetry of things and practices—of nature, craft, and art entrusted to the care of humans. Human skill commensurates with the commanding presence of a thing, and human devotion corresponds to the profound coherence of the thing with the world.

To modern and hypermodern sensibility, focal things appear scattered and forlorn. The modern observer is struck by the absence of a systematic order and principled justification. The hypermodern spectator is disappointed by the lack of glamour. But to people inspired by focal things and engaged in focal practices, the absence of cogency is the postmodern sign of life and the lack of glitter is the mark of reality. Such is postmodern realism. Although it comes to life in bodily engagement, communal celebration, and focal orientation, the latter is yet a precarious affair.

People engaged in focal practices gratefully acknowledge the immediate and centering power of the focal thing they are devoted to. You cannot remain unmoved by the gentleness and conformation of a well-bred and well-trained horse—more than a thousand pounds of big-boned, well-muscled animal, slick of coat and sweet of smell, obedient and mannerly, and yet forever a menace with its innocent power and ineradicable inclination to seek refuge in flight; and always a burden with its need to be fed, wormed, and shod, with its liability to cuts and infections, to laming and heaves. But when it greets you with a nicker, nuzzles your chest, and regards you with a large and liquid eye, the question of where you want to be and what you want to do has been answered.

It has been settled for the moment since the reproach of truancy rests on the answer.[14] The focal area of the horse can seem like a charmed island floating in a universe of technology. This is no longer "a world of hand and horse and hand tools and horse tools."[15] If focal charms are as ungrounded as hyperreal thrills, one is simply the melancholy sibling of the other. But focal things are in fact grounded in the underlying reality, and focal practices are heirs to immemorial traditions. There are, at any rate, precarious roots and bonds of this sort. Postmodern realists at times lose heart when faced with the isolation of focal things and the diaspora of focal practices. Wherever their paths cross, however, they recognize each other and feel the kinship of the focused life. Musicians recognize gardeners; horse people understand artisans.

The experience of this kinship is encouraging because it lifts the sense of confinement that can overtake a focal concern. It opens up a wider reality that allows one to refocus one's life when failing strength or changing circumstances withdraw a focal thing. It also provides for a dwelling place marked out by the configuration of several focal things, not only by things of nature, craft, and art, but also by athletics, the culture of the table, the culture of the word, and by worship. Worship, of course, is not just one among many focal points. As hypermodernism threatens postmodern realism with mortal distraction, religion disquiets it with the claim of totality.

PATIENT VIGOR   If parents could give their children an attitude but had to choose between sullenness
and hyperactivity, no doubt they would prefer hyperactivity. We want
our children to be equal to the challenges of their time, to excel and to
prosper in their pursuits, and to lead vigorous and enjoyable lives. Sullen people have been barred from the excitement at the center of the
contemporary arena and from the spoils of the battles that are being
fought there. At the same time, they have despaired of the struggle
with the hardness of reality and have grown insensible to the challenges of things that need to be done. If they do not leave their houses
unpainted and their hedges untrimmed, they do leave their tables un-
set, their books unread, their stories untold, their songs unsung, and
their children unattended. Yet hyperactivity represents a counterfeit
vigor and joy. While parents may be relieved that a hyperactive child
has gained the rewards and approval of contemporary society, they feel
more sorrow than pride when they see the substance of life consumed
in a blaze of exertion and ambition.

In the third generation, recollection of the bracing effect that
the hardness of life had in the Great Depression seems to be fading.
Grandparents look at their descendants with uncomprehending dis-
may if the latter are sullen, with troubled approval if they are hyperactive. The venerable prescription of relentless work seems to be
scorned by the sullen and misunderstood by the hyperactive. It is, in
fact, inapplicable to the final crisis of the modern project. The penulti-
mate crisis, the Great Depression, was overcome through one more
rally of the army of modernism.[16] Totalitarianism abroad required a
forcible reply, and the need to prevail regardless of resistance was in
step with the dedication to the norm of regardless power in its modern
version—the determination to prevail aggressively regardless of
physical resistance, to prevail methodically regardless of complexity,
and to prevail socially regardless of traditions.

Regardless power has been the leading edge of modern technology. It has also been the way of life of everyone who has had the full
franchise in the technological society. All of us exercise this sort of
power through the switches, keys, and dials that allow us to summon
up, regardless of time, place, skill, or strength, whatever our hearts desire. Though regardless power may live on in its refined hypermodern

incarnation, the brute and arrogant offspring of modernism has lost its vitality and credibility.

If sullenness needs redemption, hyperactivity rejection, and regardless power retirement, what is the proper response to the postmodern condition? Postmodern reality, no less than its modern ancestor, is hard. Its hardness shows itself in duress and firmness. The duress of reality comes home to us in pain and adversity. We feel the firmness of reality when it inspires and invigorates us. Our particular causes of duress today are the limits of the land, the hostility of people, and the frailty of the body. The classic modern reply to these burdens has been the technological fix. Mass production and automation were to be technological fixes for social injustice, the hydrogen bomb for belligerence, the IUD for sexual profligacy, nuclear desalination plants for wastefulness, computers and communication technology for inept teaching, and safer cars for careless driving.[17]

There is a grain of truth in this. Technology is part of the postmodern destiny, and the flow of its benefits should not be stopped or spurned. It would be heartless to dump the premodern burden of sexuality on women and fanatic to reject scientific and technical sophistication in dealing with water problems. But it is also part of the postmodern experience that the duress of reality should not be subjected entirely to hard solutions. The crucial task, however, is not simply to put up with the recalcitrance of reality sullenly and resentfully but to endure it bravely if not gladly.

Patience shows greater strength than power. When power prevails in its paradigmatic modern form, it establishes order on the ruins of inconvenient circumstances and on the suppression of uncooperative people. Regardless power rests on destruction and remains haunted by it. Patience has the time and strength to recognize complicated conditions and difficult people, to engage them in cooperation and conversation. The powerful provoke envy and fear; the patient earn admiration and affection. By patience I do not mean passivity but endurance, the kind of strength we admire in an athlete who is equal to the length of a run or the trials of a game.

As regards the environment, the task of postmodern patience is to endure the limits of the land. This country is blessed with an extraordinarily rich and spacious continent. Our inability to live more nearly with the energy it yields and with its capacity for wastes bespeaks an impatient and immature culture. The nation's impatience with its poor and helpless likewise shows a juvenile sort of self-righteousness. While people of liberal persuasion will feel free of the taint of social impatience, at least in principle, none of us is spared the ultimate test of patience when we meet with people who clearly mean us ill and give regardlessness a menacing edge. Patience has its limit, of course, when it comes to protecting our elementary welfare. But in the vicinity of that limit there is much informal and yet deeply troubling hostility. In this area patience can no longer be demanded, but it can be lived.

The frailty of our bodies, too, calls for social and individual patience. This country is terribly confused about health care—about its advancement, distribution, and financial support. There is little hope of clarification until we learn a common and, indeed, communal patience with the pains of fatal diseases, the debilities of old age, and the aches and pains of daily life. It is an eminently postmodern task because any aggressive, universal, and individualistic design to enforce a willingness to suffer is at worst doomed from the start or imposed on a resentful public at best. Only a shared understanding will encourage the individual to endure and society to agree on explicit and reasoned limits to medical intervention. More properly put, it is only when society becomes something like a community and the individual more of a member in that community that health and patience will be reconciled.[18]

Patience is needed to endure reality, yet patience itself needs a source of strength. At times we admire patience and wish we had it while being weak with impatience and anger. Not that the patient person will easily lose his or her patience. Being a moral virtue, patience, like its athletic sibling endurance, is a habitual skill, acquired gradually and maintained through exercise. The difficulty lies in the beginning and, once we have begun, in persisting when conditions are trying and bleak. What inspires us to set out for athletic endurance and to keep after it in the face of adversity is the prospect of graceful ease, the balance between the demanding feat and human competence.[19]

Similarly, the reward of patience is vigor when, having endured the duress of reality, our strength is graced and confirmed by real splendor. This is true of the artisan who, having established his craft through long training and longer hours, delights in filing strips of bamboo with "a look of concentration and serenity—the look of a man deriving intense satisfaction from his work."[20] This is true of the rider who, having endlessly trained her horse and nursed him through cuts and strangles, takes pride in his calmness when she saddles and mounts him, in his collected gait and fine response when she ever so slightly moves the reins or shifts her weight.

Vigorous people reflect the firmness of reality, the resistance and dignity of things that challenge us in a clear and present way. Just as focal things are deep and definite, so vigor is calm and articulate. The radiance of reality inspires vigor and invigorates patience. Most of us, obviously, do not have the gifts or the settings that are needed for crafts or horses to focus our lives. It would be petty to dismiss the patient vigor of the artisan or the horse owner. But it would be smug as well to overlook the limited and precarious condition of these focal things. The focal power of a thing is denied and mocked if the thing is secluded and surrounded entirely by hypermodern technology. A thing must draw its vitality from an underlying reality. If there is no such grounding, a focal thing will eventually float off into hyperspace. Thus the postmodern condition calls for greater patience and more common vigor than a limited focal practice can grant. We must acquire the patience to locate and nurture focal things within the typical postmodern setting.

COMMUNAL CELEBRATION
Postmodernism and Community

Having left modernism behind us, we now have to decide whether to proceed on the endless and joyless plain of hypermodernism or to cross over to another and more real world. For this country in particular, the latter task comes to settling down in the land that has come to be ours, to give up the restless search for a hyperreal elsewhere, and to come to terms with nature and tradition in a patient and vigorous way. The ecology and economy of postmodern realism are clear enough in broad outline. Large parts of the design are familiar from the programs of mainstream ecologists and economists. We must reduce pollution and energy consumption. We must preserve what is still wild in nature and rehabilitate what has been abused. We must put our common house in order by being more parsimonious, more careful with the infrastructure, more dedicated to research and development, more cooperative in our pursuits, more concerned about the skills of our workers.

But all of this is compatible with a mindless and unjust social order. The emerging postmodern economy can develop smoothly into hypermodernism, a culturally vacuous and socially insensitive design. Just as modern aggressiveness will not restore vigor to hypermodern vacuity, so modern liberalism will not redress the social injustice of hypermodernism. Orthodox liberalism has been left behind with modernism.[21] To invite the poor into the common order of postmodernism, two things need to be done. The first is to provide good work, enough work for everyone, and to give everyone the education required for good work. Orthodox liberals, more than anyone else, support this element of social justice, but they have been unsuccessful in securing it because they reject so dogmatically the other element needed to forge an inclusive communal order: the very idea of a community. Without a sense of community, the issue of good work for all will never be put on the political agenda. Quantity and quality of work will remain at the mercy of hypermodern consumption. There are good reasons, of course, to be wary of the exclusive and oppressive tendencies of community. The liberal apprehensions need to be answered, but they should not prevail as a peremptory challenge to a communal order.

Partisan republicans are sympathetic to the idea of a community, and philosophical republicans make it central to their political vision. The latter, especially, are concerned to restore selflessness and social cohesion to the common order. The postmodern economy, with its rejection of rigid hierarchy and ideological individualism, appears to favor republican communitarianism. But as a rule, communitarians do not avail themselves of these ambiguous bits of support. Far less have they been ready to propose a concrete social design.[22] Hence, in theory, they have been easy prey for liberal critics who charge that vagueness is the price of escaping the intrinsically oppressive tendency of any community. In practice, hypermodernism threatens to subvert communitarianism. Since republican theorists have provided neither an incisive critique of modern technology nor a real counterproposal, hypermodern technology is left to specify what remains vague in communitarianism. The premodern village is still one of the clearest instances of community. Communitarians have no reply when the hyperreal, hyperactive, and hyperintelligent global village is offered as the contemporary instantiation of community.

Postmodern ecology, economy, and community need to be grounded and centered in reality if they are to resist hypermodern disorientation and desiccation. The underlying reality of the postmodern era comes most vigorously to the fore in the provinces, vigorously there and then, marginally and precariously in relation to the dominant contemporary culture. The latter is inescapably urban and indeed megalopolitan as Lawrence Haworth has pointed out:

> City and country once signified two distinct styles of life, and the nation was two nations side by side. This is no longer true: the two styles are coalescing into one, in the same way that all classes are moving into the middle class. The truer image is that of a nation becoming urban, not merely in the sense that cities are growing outward, but in the deeper social sense that styles of life are becoming uniform, and uniformly urban. Megalopolis is a vanguard.[23]

Unless we are able to discover and nourish in the community and in the city those focal things and practices that are thriving in the family and in the country, the underlying reality of the postmodern era will languish everywhere. The symmetry that obtains in the small between a focal thing and a vigorous person joined in a focal practice needs to be discovered and recovered in the large. The larger symmetry will show up as a public affirmation of the underlying postmodern reality.

One may hope to help the practical task along through theoretical illumination. If such illumination is to comprehend the entire public sphere, it must evidently be comprehensive. Comprehensiveness, in turn, must command a suitably general if not universal vocabulary. But if we satisfy that requirement, we fall back on the discourse of modernism. The problem is more than a matter of style. It concerns the danger that in our attempt to demonstrate the presence and significance of reality universally, we miss it altogether. We must meet reality on its own particular and proper terms.

Particularism has been hailed as the hallmark of postmodernism.[24] How particular is particular discourse? It is closest to reality when it is brought down to proper names. In speaking of urban life, I will properly talk about Missoula, Montana. If it is far from exemplary and typical, so much the better. It is undeniably real. And yet, if the anecdotal and the arbitrary, the genteel variants of hypermodern discontinuity and disposability, are to be avoided, there must be greater coherence and depth. As a matter of fact, all that is real hangs together in being surrounded by technology and threatened by hypermodernism. Underneath that enveloping and perilous coherence is the unforethinkable kinship of reality. Postmodern realism is to comprehend modernism and hypermodernism through a schematic account, thus providing a clearing where reality can come to be present in a narrative recounting. Hence, postmodern discourse is properly narrative, but it is also schematic when it comes to general features and generic traits.

To begin with a general reminder, modernism has been the enemy of real urbanity. The catalyst of destruction was the automobile. It furnished the rationale for clearing away the untidy urban fabric and replacing it with a pseudopastoral landscape of towers in a park. It provided the vehicle for the upper and middle classes to seek a pseudo-rustic setting in the suburbs. The modern program failed to succeed entirely, yet it succeeded well enough to blight city centers and to forestall constructive solutions to the plight of the lower class.

Missoula never had many residents at its center. The residential districts used to surround and support a center of stores, banks, businesses, bars, restaurants, hotels, and railroad stations. Under the centrifugal pull of the automobile, the center failed to hold. The suburbs spread out so far that it became impossible to walk into town, and it was inconvenient to drive there. Shopping centers with ample parking sprang up in the suburbs. Businesses set up shop along the highways at the edge of town. In 1978, Missoula got its shopping mall, a pleasant brick structure amidst fine landscaping and a grand circle of mountain ranges and peaks. Once inside, however, you are anywhere and nowhere.

Meanwhile, businesses in town closed. The railroad stations succumbed to the interstate highway and the airport. Downtown became ever more deserted and desolate. In 1980, the Missoula City Council found downtown to be blighted and, as provided by state law, designated it a tax increment district; the property taxes that accrued to the city, the county, and the school districts were frozen at 1978 levels and all increases due to rising property values would flow to the Missoula Redevelopment Agency. The initial trickle grew into a healthy stream of money, which was channeled by the agency to buy up dilapidated property and offer it for development, to rehabilitate old buildings, and to beautify downtown with awnings, plazas, and plantings. New buildings for banks and law firms went up; parking was increased; the city center seemed on its way to becoming a center for professional services.

In New York, Chicago, Boston, and Seattle, decay and renewal took place on a much more dramatic scale. High-rise buildings and urban shopping malls are prominent landmarks of restructuring.[25] But an air of unreality clings to such renovation. Mixed-used skyscrapers and carefully designed urban malls are self-centered little universes that turn their backs on the real city. Thoughtful observers find these constructions controlled, contrived, artificial, and superficial—most disturbingly so when historical structures are preserved as facades and shells for the most recent and refined forms of consumption. It is urban hyperreality that troubles these critics.[26]

The Daily City   Thank God, however, the real postmodern city is alive and asserting itself against hyperreal subversion. If we may borrow from the vocabulary of the church calendar, we can call the two sides of urban reality the ferial and festal, the common reality of daily life and the festive reality of celebration.

Jane Jacobs has been the patron saint of the city's daily reality. Her intercessions have broken the force of the modernist assault on the urban texture of enjoyable city life. The woof and warp of that fabric are the streets, interlaced in a grid of small city blocks. Street life is real in its commanding presence and continuity with time and place. It commands our attention and affection because it prospers of its own accord and proceeds in its own rhythm. Street life can be favored, and it can certainly be destroyed, but it cannot be controlled.

Missoula was founded when late in 1864 C. P. Higgins, Frank Worden, and David Pattee built a sawmill a little ways west of where Rattlesnake Creek flows into the Clark Fork River. The following year they built a flour mill and moved a store to the same site alongside the Mullan Road that connected the Missouri to the Columbia. Hotels, shops, and homes followed. An irregular grid of streets emerged. Missoula began to prosper.[27] Urban life emerges and flourishes when a diversity of human concerns converges and continues to cohere along and across streets. You cannot design or control city life; you can let it happen and contribute to it by allowing stores and residences, manufacturing and retailing, the utilitarian and the extravagant to coexist.

A street exhibits an unfolded and understandable order. The bakery and its owner are distinguished from the grocer and the grocery. We smell the bread baking; we see the produce being trucked in. In a supermarket, to the contrary, all underlying distinctions and connections are consolidated and concealed. We are left with a superficial display of commodities. Street life has its circadian and seasonal rhythms. The street wakes up in the morning with a spurt of busyness, relaxes in mid-morning, gathers momentum toward noon, calms down once more in the afternoon, becomes roily between the end of work and dinner, and settles into a steady pace of activities in the evening. Street life tends to be lazier in the summer, bracing in the fall, restrained in the winter, and exuberant in the spring.[28] In a well-lit, air-conditioned, twenty-four-hour supermarket, however, time decays to a featureless flow that feebly reflects the changes of the real world outside.

Street life in Missoula never expired entirely. In the seventies, it lived on in scattered bars, restaurants, and shops. The urban texture was tattered and torn, however. In the eighties it began to regenerate. Stores began to fill the vacancies, buildings were restored to the grand aspirations of an earlier time. Lately Missoula has begun to loosen the straitjacket of the early modern extractive industry that has been the bane of Montana and to fashion a postmodern economy.[29] The timber industry is declining in Missoula; crafts, small-scale production, light manufacturing, specialized horticulture, and professional services are growing.

People have returned to the city center to work and to shop, to eat and to talk, to walk and to look. Of course, the urban fabric of a small town is a loose and casual garment compared with the tight and stylish attire of a metropolis. Missoula has nothing like the intricate and pulsing life of Hudson Street, beloved of Jane Jacobs, or the messy and captivating vitality of Lexington Avenue, beloved of William Whyte.[30] The sidewalks of Missoula are never congested; in the evenings and on weekends they are empty. But Missoula does have pleasantly crowded times and places. The northern end of Higgins Avenue leads up to the stately neo-Renaissance building of the former Northern Pacific Railroad station, now housing a restaurant and small brewery. Just to the east of it the city has set aside part of an old brick-paved street for the farmers' market that is held there during the summer on Tuesday evenings and Saturday mornings. Between a monument to Captain Mullan and one of the steam locomotives that helped to make his divide-crossing road obsolete, nearly a hundred growers, bakers, and coffee makers offer their goods to a leisurely crowd. Prominent among the growers are the Hmong who, having fled the highlands of Vietnam, excel at raising vegetables in the Missoula Valley. There is a little stage, sometimes occupied by musicians, always bordered by coffee drinkers sitting on its steps. People talk more than they shop, knitting up the raveled edges of the social fabric. How are the children doing? How is the summer going? Can you make that meeting? Have you heard that Don is thinking of retirement? Have you met Claire? She has just moved here; she's a writer. The useful and the playful are woven together.

So they are on Wednesdays at noon, three quarters of a mile south, where Higgins Avenue crosses the Clark Fork River. A small amphitheater, set against the grass and trees of the riverbank, opens on a tiled plaza. A band is playing there, surrounded by the tables and carts of thirty or so food vendors. Fifteen hundred Missoulians are having lunch here, listening to the music, talking and being talked to, watching and being watched.

In the context of technological concealment and hypermodern flimsiness, daily city life has an engaging sturdiness and comprehensibility, an order that has been familiar to humanity for thousands of years. Here are real spaces, bounded, shaped, inhabitable, and traversable. Here are real persons, talking with their faces, hands, feet, their clothing and their jewelry. Here are real tasks, taking shirts to the laundry, getting a baguette at the bakery, buying a paper at the newsstand. The ferial city favors a bodily vigorous, richly connected, and securely oriented life. Vigor, orientation, and connectedness, however, need to be extended. If real urbanity is restricted to islands of daily energy and diversity, the tides of hypermodernism will erode its foundation, and ferial urbanity will either collapse or float off into hyperreality. Daily reality needs to be linked to the natural, raised to the festal, and extended to the poor.

A bit of nature—trees and flowers—enlivens the daily city; a lot of nature—expanses of grass, bushes, and trees—kills it. The street is like the interior of a house writ large. It is a traditional and human setting of high concentration and interaction. The ferial must not be mixed with the natural, but it should be connected to it. It should contain parks, and it should be linked to rural and wild nature by trails. The Milwaukee Road used to occupy the south shore of the Clark Fork. When it went bankrupt, the city acquired the property and turned it into a park that has a trail running through the entire town and on its eastern side continuing through Hellgate Canyon up the river. Parks and trails are being pieced together on the north shore as well. One of the pieces is Caras Park where Missoulians lunch on the Wednesdays of summer. Another trail is forming along Rattlesnake Creek, a northern tributary of the Clark Fork. After seven miles the trail enters the Rattlesnake National Recreation Area; after eight miles more it reaches the Rattlesnake Wilderness Area.

Larger cities have longer trails.[31] In each case, however, a real connection is made from the city to the country. People experience the transition from the urban to the rural not as a change of scenery that passes by on a screen or behind a windshield, but through bodily vigor, moving step by step from the built to the growing environment. Runners and walkers know more intimately the lay of the land, the direction of the wind, and the course of the sun, and so they are oriented more broadly in their world.[32]

The Festive City   When experts are convened to consider public life in the cities, they often find it scattered, disoriented, or altogether deceased.[33] This is in part because they overlook the ferial side of it. In part, however, they simply confront the ravages of modernism. The eminent domain of the public realm has been sacrificed to the instrumentalities of technology, to transportation and storage, to expressways and high rises. But even in its better half, the diagnosis fails to be clear-sighted, as is evident from the experts' uncertainty as to what exactly is missing. The best remedy they can usually think of is a spatially extended and theatrically heightened version of the daily city, busier and more ostentatious kinds of walking and talking, dressing and moving, selling and buying, collected and amassed in a square or plaza.[34]

However, the final realization of public life happens not in a hyperactive elevation of the daily but in festive celebration. Such celebrations need not and could not be designed and produced. They are alive in athletics, the arts, and religion. The reason they escape attention is their precarious and sometimes corrupted state. Guided by the pattern of technology, we have taken sustained and sophisticated measures to mechanize and commodify celebration, to transfer the burden of enactment to a powerful and concealed machinery and leave the participants with a commodity guaranteed to excite and entertain.[35] As technology advances on celebration, the elements of genuine celebration—reality, community, and divinity—are weakened and eventually expelled.

Reality in athletics is spare but crucial. To play baseball, all you need is a smooth and level field, four bases, a bat, and a ball. For a fine game, however, that reality must be guarded against corruption. The bases must be properly spaced, the ball must have the right size and bounce, the bat must have its solidity and weight. The core reality is respected and defended in organized baseball; without it, the game would become a farce. Yet all too often the real core has been isolated and impoverished by a hyperreal environment, by astroturf and a domed, air-conditioned enclosure. The game becomes a pleasant commodity. The spectators become customers.

Recently, a thirst for reality and a sense of community have asserted themselves in Baltimore. When the Baltimore Orioles decided to build a new baseball stadium, they did not pick an open space outside of the city as a landing site for an enclosed, air-conditioned, and astroturfed spacecraft that could have descended just as plausibly on Frankfurt to contain soccer or on Tokyo to accommodate sumo wrestling. Rather, they cooperated with city and state authorities and decided to build at the edge of downtown on the site of an abandoned rail yard, replacing public utility with public pleasure. The site is bounded on one side by a huge and venerable brick warehouse. Rather than tearing it down, the architects have incorporated it as a backdrop for right field and as a space for offices. The stadium itself will respond to the masonry of the warehouse with its brick arches. It will recall the character of the old beloved city stadiums in Chicago, Detroit, and Boston. It will be open to the sights of downtown Baltimore as well as to wind, rain, and sun. Games will be played on grass. When you sit in the stands, you cannot doubt that here is Baltimore, this is summer, and a game of venerable traditions is being played.[36]

A rich reality is needed to sponsor a sense of community. A thoughtful and graceful ballpark tunes people to the same harmonies. It inspires common pride and pleasure, a shared sense of season and place, a joint anticipation of drama. Given such attunement, banter and laughter flow naturally across strangers and unite them into a community. When reality and community conspire this way, divinity descends on the game, divinity of an impersonal and yet potent kind. At the beginning of a real game, there is no way of predicting or controlling what will happen. No one can produce or guarantee the flow of a game. It unfolds and reveals itself in the playing. It inspires grace and despair, it provokes heroics and failure, it infuses enthusiasm and inflicts misery. It is always greater than the individuals it unites.

The Flatheads, Kootenais, and Pend d'Oreilles who gather on the reservation at the Arlee Powwow in early June mill about and sit around casually, showing the benefits and curses of the white man's dress, food, liquor, and tobacco no less than the Caucasian visitors.

But when they sit down to the stick game, a quiet excitement rises, and the spirit that graces players with the power to conceal and the power to see is among them. When they gather around the drum to chant and play, vigor and splendor infuse them.

The holy game of baseball is thriving in Missoula, from the American Legion team by way of the City Parks and Recreation leagues to Little League and pickup games. Baseball is vigorous and widespread. Great celebration needs to be more powerfully focused, however. It draws its strength from the number of people whose attendance and attention it commands. A minor league team would gather and focus the public life of Missoula, and center and heighten its sense of community. Just as the project of a new ballpark has captured the imagination of Baltimore, so the idea of bringing a professional team to Missoula has inspired enthusiasm and cooperation in all quarters. These people are not interested in a project of community building. It is the thing, its charms and traditions, that have captivated their good will. Community gathers around reality.

But reality also challenges the community. Where to build the ballpark? Out in the open on the outskirts, tediously tied to the city by strings of cars? The receding modern economy has given Baltimore an abandoned railroad yard for its ballpark. It has left Missoula with a site once occupied by a lumber mill just west of the river park on the south side of the Clark Fork. It is within walking distance of downtown and its parking lots and bordered by residential districts. A ballpark at that location would strengthen the urban fabric; the games, played in the evenings and on weekends, would invigorate city life at just the times it now lapses into torpor. But the downtown site is the more expensive one and requires more dedication.

No matter how deep our dedication, baseball constitutes a limited realm. It is a rich and graceful world, to be sure, well tended by some of our finest writers, but it is a predominantly male world. It cares little about marriage, about birth and death, even less about distant times and cultures. Art, to the contrary, is mindful of all this, embodying it in words, songs, movements, and things that focus and illuminate the world at large. The health of art, too, is indicated by the vigor of reality, community, and divinity.

Even more than athletics, art has been subverted by technology.

At pop music concerts, reality is torn apart into a gigantic, intricate staging machinery and an alluring, hypercharged commodity. Avant-garde art has marked out its place in society through the exclusion or contempt of community. While popular art is too shallow an abode for divinity, high art is too constricted a construction. Between these depressing extremes there is a blessed variety of real and communal art. Missoulians have invited and celebrated it at the international choral festivals held in 1987 and 1990. Choirs from Scotland, Lithuania, Germany, Italy, Uruguay, Great Falls, and elsewhere convened and sang in dozens of places to thousands of people. Their music extended from the popular to the artful, from the sentimental to the severe, from the secular to the sacred. The singers gathered a world that was wider and deeper than any World Series, a world that contained more sorrow and joy than the most stirring game.

For a week Missoula was a community of celebration; the energy of the town was centered in music. But then the energy was gone, especially the energy of the core group of inspired citizens who had organized the event. They put the festival together despite lack of staff, funding, and housing. They made up for all these deficiencies with grit and paid for them with exhaustion. After two years of recovery, they will gather their strength again, or so they did once.

During the interval, art is not dead in Missoula. There are indigenous and regular poetry readings, art exhibits, symphony performances, and chamber concerts. Missoula is a sporting and artful town. Athletics and the arts, both fine and liberal, are securely woven into the urban texture. Athletics, moreover, joins the built and the natural environment of Missoula. A river runs through it and invites fishing, floating, and swimming. Emerald borders of cottonwoods and grass run alongside it and contain running trails, playing fields, a swimming pool. Some day, perhaps, they will contain a ballpark. Runners, hikers, bikers, and skiers shuttle between the town and the mountains.

Missoula was too insignificant a challenge for the transformations of modernism and has kept most of its genteel architecture. At its eastern end, in the nook of the portal of Hellgate Canyon and the Clark Fork, it is home to a university with a school of music and a school of fine arts. It is the residence of numerous accomplished writers. But the fate of communal celebration still hangs in the balance.

The acquisition and location of a professional baseball team do. The choral festival does. The city, moreover, is looking at the old Milwaukee Station on the south side of Higgins Bridge and at the Wilma Theatre on the north side. The former, a handsome neo-Romanesque building, now facing the river park, has failed as a restaurant. The latter, Missoula's only palatial movie theater and festive auditorium, may retire from public life with its present owner. Between decay and commercial development, the city must find a way to secure these landmarks for communal celebration.

Communal These problems look insignificant and even
Politics quaint when set off against the oppressive
reality—the destruction, violence, and poverty—of the inner cities in metropolitan areas. It would be arrogant to dismiss the endeavors of city officials and social workers to contain and alleviate this misery. Postmodern realism, however, offers New York and Missoula the same task—the care of communal celebrations. That care is at the center of communal politics. Its task is to take up the burden modernism has despaired of, the obligations of justice, as well as to counter the hypermodern specter constructively.

To begin with the latter task, the issue is not so much prevention of hypermodernism as fidelity to realism. Since as citizens we are involved unavoidably in fundamental material decisions, we must see to it that these decisions are made so that communal celebrations are affirmed publicly. Through political action we must make sure that arts and athletics are given central and festive structures and locations in our communities, that they have the staff they need to set the stage for communal celebration.

In theory, both conservatives and liberals want to leave this task to voluntary associations, the conservatives because they will be the ones who primarily control and enjoy such associations, the liberals because they want government to remain neutral when it comes to the pursuit of excellence. But in practice the question inevitably is not *whether* but *how* the government should involve itself in shaping the tangible and morally decisive setting of common life. And in practice the government underwrites, assists, or facilitates sports arenas, playing fields, museums, concert halls, athletic programs, art and music academies.

What we need is not radical innovation but a vigorous shift from promoting the hypermodern machinery to supporting places where reality, community, and divinity are joined in celebration. Though Missoula needs diverse commercial development to thicken and quicken the urban tissue, it rightly has refused to surrender the riverfront to commercialism. It has preserved one landmark for communal celebration by helping the Missoula Children's Theatre to acquire the vacant Central School building, and it may save and even establish other centers of celebration.

Pennsylvania Station was razed in 1963. Five years later, the New York City Landmarks Preservation Commission was established. Since then, celebratory structures have been saved and restored, some by private enterprise, others by the city. Though New York's record of public stewardship has been fair for buildings, it has been poor for land. The creation of Battery Park City preserved public spaces along the Hudson River, but the former Pennsylvania Railroad yards and the land under the New York Coliseum were unceremoniously left to private interests.[37]

It is plain that without vigorous support places of public celebration will remain marginal to the urban setting. But even where government acts forcefully to preserve landmarks and create public spaces, the results too often leave us disappointed. Either the stately historic structures have exactly the same commercial, bureaucratic, or consumptive content as their tacky modern siblings or the well-intended public spaces remain empty. Even the best planned projects fail to keep their promises.[38] Richard Sennett complains:

> Our culture is suffering from a surfeit of sameness. Take Battery Park City, lower Manhattan's recent large-scale development, which was built to look like more of the city rather than as an isolated project. It is neutral and homogeneous. Its social failure is painfully apparent; the public spaces inside and outside its buildings are almost always empty.[39]

Of course, some places of public celebration are by their very nature empty most of the time, like ballparks and concert halls; some, like parks, are empty part of the time. One must distinguish between daily enjoyment and festive celebration and must recognize the continuum between them. Streets, courts, gardens, squares, plazas, fountains, and monuments are at their best continually busy places where people sit, talk, eat, read, and enjoy their city. Enjoyment rises to small-scale celebration when street musicians, jugglers, or magicians show up and a little community of celebration gathers around the performers. Daily enjoyment and celebration, too, need more resolute and generous municipal support. Cities must prevail on businesses to make their premises hospitable, and they have to protect street people from their ancient adversaries, the merchants.[40] In fact, government should assure a festive setting and comfortable seating for street music and provide staff for auditioning and scheduling where demand suggests it. The city must serve the musicians and listeners, however, not try to control and arrange things.

That still leaves government with the most difficult and important task, the support of festal and focused celebration. For just as the sites of celebration are confined to marginality without public support, so the enactment of many celebrations is threatened with instability if left to private resources. Communal celebrations that enjoy stability are never private in more than name anyway. Corporate gifts, municipal facilities, and tax advantages involve the public directly and indirectly in the support of symphonies, museums, and ball clubs. But much more needs to be done. The choral festival in Missoula will be an intermittent and precarious affair until the public, through city government, makes a fundamental decision to sustain it.

When celebratory communitarianism gets on the political agenda, one cannot fairly expect it to be less contentious than curbs-and-gutters liberalism.[41] In any case, celebration will constitute a more substantial topic of public debate than curbs and gutters. We must be careful, however, not to employ modernist strategies in getting celebration on the postmodern agenda. One should not try to devise mechanisms and procedures designed to guarantee the selection and funding of celebrations once and for all.[42] The politics of postmodern realism is devoted ad hoc, to this particular community of celebration and then to that. Missoula's City Council was glad to spend ten thousand dollars to study the possibility of taking on a golf course, yet it agonized endlessly over spending a fifth of that amount to create a cultural commission. To proceed systematically is to borrow the weapons of liberalism only to be defeated by the prejudices of liberalism. At length, to be sure, vigorous citizenship requires that the public conversation be equal to public practices. The public needs to become conscious and confident of communal celebration so that it may achieve through citizenship what is unattainable through consumership.

Naturally, the question of tolerance and evenhandedness will be raised vehemently when the public conversation turns to communal celebration. Why support a choral festival rather than a jazz festival? Why music rather than a golf tournament? What about the interests of the snowmobilers? Liberal critics of communitarianism quickly rise above such particular questions and roundly condemn communitarianism as easy prey for the Torquemadas, Stalins, Hitlers, and Pol Pots. They point, with better reason, to current instances of racial, religious, and ethnic strife.[43] The first reply to liberals is the reminder that government is never neutral in the moral construction of the common order. Hypermodernism is no less prejudicial to postmodern realism than vice versa. Racial or religious divisions themselves are often no more than pretexts for the unequal distribution of technological affluence.

There are more constructive replies, however. Focal realism, the starting point of communal celebration, is an antidote to fanaticism in itself. People who have been captivated by music make their children take lessons; they invite their neighbors and urge their friends to go to concerts. They will make music themselves, but they will not exclude the runners or condemn the writers. In fact, they may run and write themselves or have spouses or acquaintances who do. There is an interlacing of communities of celebration that provides for a community of communities rather than a society of sects.[44]

Still, government must exercise vigilance in curbing zealotry and invidiousness. There should be at least two principles of public support for communities of celebration—open membership and contestable funding. Open membership means that anyone, regardless of class or race, can join a community as long as he or she is devoted to what the community celebrates.[45] At the powwow in Arlee, there are always some white people, usually men, who are so taken with the splendor of the Native Americans' costumes and the power of their dances that they, too, dress up and dance. With gentle mockery, their tribal affiliation is given by the Native Americans and by the white dancers themselves as Wannabee. Still, when it comes to Indian culture, the Native Americans are bearers of a unique gift and burden.

The Arlee Powwow does not receive direct public funding. It is open out of generosity. Any community, however, that does receive public support must be open as a matter of principle. Moreover, it should explain itself and its expenditures of public funds regularly, always reckoning with the possibility that those funds may be withheld. The political task is to maintain the delicate balance between stability and accountability. There is no formula that will guarantee this balance, nor one that will settle once and for all which communities will receive support and which will not. Why is the choral festival a good candidate for public support in Missoula? Because Missoula has a university with a school of music. The choral conductor there has great vision and energy, and he has galvanized the community. This is the substance of the situation. In postmodern realism, substance informs procedure.

Open membership in communities of celebration provides a new opening for justice, and so, to be sure, does the public care of the daily enjoyment of city life. New openings are needed because the liberal pursuit of justice has been stalled. Of course, to think of justice as a kind of equality is itself the signal and precious bequest of modern liberalism to postmodern realism. More particularly, John Rawls has provided an admirably circumspect and compassionate design of liberal justice. But it has failed to inspire enthusiasm outside the academy, and while it all but bans public support for communities of celebration, it is entirely open to hypermodern specification and subversion.[46]

Liberal justice is perilously incomplete. Still, it should be corrected and completed rather than abandoned. Instead of narrowing all our energy to the advancement of civic membership by way of formal rights and fair opportunities, we ought to realize that civic membership is substantively and actually enacted in communal celebration. Here the rich are not helping the poor; they join them.[47] Community is a personal relationship that is positioned fruitfully between private intimacy and public anonymity. Intimacy joins relatives and friends who share moral convictions and economic circumstances. Intimacy is faked when extended to larger groups, fraudulent when pretended between rich and poor.[48] Anonymity is the relation among the individuals in a mass society who share no more than economic and political instrumentalities, utilities, and bureaucracies. Anonymity has made it easy for the rich to ignore the poor.

Community is a relation of good will on definite terms. In a community of celebration, the terms are defined by the reality being celebrated. When people join for Saturday morning softball games on Chicago's lakefront, they do not pretend to share their possessions or beliefs; they have gathered just to play. Though the boundaries of the field and the rules constitute the limits of their cooperation, it is a rich and rewarding thing that has been marked out. It invites people to disclose their grit and their grace, their valor and their humor. And if things go well, enthusiasm invigorates and unites them.

The Heavenly These people will carry some of their
City enthusiasm with them to their various social stations. A community of celebration radiates festivity and coherence into society. It is focal by nature; it radiates as well as it collects. It gathers the past as it does for the middle-aged softball player who, poised at the plate, recollects and impersonates Ernie Banks; it opens up the future to the young catcher who emulates Carlton Fisk. Baseball with its love of records and statistics, its broadly based and highly tiered organization, has perhaps more focal force than any other single institution in this county. It is a real bastion against the hypermodern hordes. While it too suffers from hyperactive attacks and hyperreal attrition, it remains a realm of real celebration. If we are equal to its commanding presence, we will act sensibly and vigorously to restrain hypermodernism.

More needs to be done, of course. Not only do we have to maintain and build more ballparks and playing fields; we must also preserve and clear central spaces in our cities for other sports, for concerts, museums, academies, for running and playing, for singing and dancing, for painting and sculpture. We should honor and practice the great things that we know well and are confident of, tennis and gymnastics, baroque music and jazz, Rembrandt and Henry Moore. But who knows what kinds of celebration will arise and where? Postmodern realism is not an ideology of platforms and programs but a matter of flexibility and cooperation.

To conclude matters in this way would be disingenuous. It would suppress a profound need and a crucial fact of communal celebration, namely religion. People feel a deep desire for comprehensive and comprehending orientation. To be human is to have a capacity for the beginning and end of all things and for assuming a position among them. For all their powerful reality, arts and athletics offer a partial view of the world as a whole and uncertain gifts for attaining a graceful and peaceful place within it. Modern theologians have attempted to demonstrate a fundamental human deficiency that can be remedied only by religion.[49] If this ever was a viable enterprise, it has expired with modernism. Now it is simply a fact that the great majority of people in this country seek orientation in religion. They must be acting from a real need, for whatever charges one may bring against the late modern era, it does not coerce or cajole people to go to church, synagogue, mosque, or temple. Yet people in the United States are more manifestly religious than democratic.[50]

This is not to say that people's needs are being well met by religion. Even raising this issue as a matter of public policy causes Americans great difficulty. We now view the First Amendment as a wall that sequesters religious issues from the public square, although neither the origin nor the wording of the amendment require this construction.[51] Whatever historical contingencies have led to erecting the wall, it has meanwhile been given a liberal foundation. The liberal contention is that only by suspending our personal beliefs can we agree on a fair and enduring social order. But if a person's final conviction is religious, then the suspension, if any, will be done by a religious person for religious reasons. If we cannot be content and confident that the suspension arises out of that person's religion, how can we either ask for it or rely on it? Am I asking, then, for a religious grounding of democracy and social justice? If there is a universal principle of postmodern political discourse, it can only be this: Let everyone speak in the first person, singular and plural.

We Christians have learned our compassion and care for everyone without exception from Christ. His example has taught us patience. His teachings are alive in the communities that go back to him. His example has ever and again been embodied in saintly persons. For us Catholics in particular, Christianity is this living community, invigorated by the celebration of the Eucharist.

The Roman Catholic Church has suffered terribly under modernism. For the first time in her history she was unable to appropriate and sanctify the surrounding culture. At first she fell back on medieval styles of thinking and building, holding the secular at arm's length while surrendering her administration to the aggressive and methodical tendencies of modernism. In the second half of this century, she threw away what cultural substance she had left while proving herself unequal to the clear spiritual and political task of accepting and redeeming democracy within her own communal order.

There is consolation, however, in the works of our Episcopalian brothers and sisters. An imposing monument to postmodern religious celebration is the Cathedral of St. John the Divine in upper Manhattan. To European eyes, it is an emblem of this country and its culture, immense and unfinished, ingenuous and vigorous. The hierarchy of the Roman Catholic Church wants to hold onto divinity while avoiding reality and slighting community. Hence the church is ailing at the center and surviving mainly at the periphery and in the diaspora. The people at St. John's have seen that divinity must become real and that art, once the daughter of religion, can now be her sister. Genuine art is the disclosure of focal reality, which is in itself divine, however tentatively. Hence the arts are housed in the cathedral and are part of the liturgy. There are companies of dancers and musicians; there are artists in residence and workshops of artisans.[52]

Divinity and reality inspire community. The principle of open membership prevails at St. John's. People of all classes, tongues, and denominations are welcome, if only they are ready to celebrate the breaking of the bread. The celebration is conducted according to the venerable Book of Common Prayer, but it has welcomed Jewish, Buddhist, Shintoist, and African devotions and sacraments. When we have been invited and invigorated by sacred celebration, we want to help the weak get up on their own two feet and join in. Opening the doors is not enough when so many cannot walk. Being sure of one's place also gives one the patience to let people walk away once they are on their feet. Divine patience will prevail in the end. Accordingly, the people of St. John's feed the hungry, shelter the homeless, build housing for the poor, and care for the young, whether they worship at the cathedral or not.[53]

A church like St. John's deserves public support. It receives indirect public assistance through its tax-exempt status and through the city funds that are used in its housing program. Generally, government is ready to aid churches in promoting social welfare; the public at large is inclined to adopt and appreciate sacred buildings.[54] Some Christians may feel misunderstood when their endeavors are assimilated to social justice and their sanctuaries to the cultural heritage. The renewal of Roman Catholicism in this country, at any rate, depends on whether it comes to terms with democratic equality and contemporary culture. This is what the postmodern spirit, the holy spirit, calls us to do. Rather than abandoning the grand churches in our inner cities, we must seek flexible cooperation with the government, with foundations, neighborhood associations, sister denominations, artists, minorities, and women's groups, according to the example of St. John the Divine.

On the Sunday afternoon of June 11, 1989, four thousand people gathered at St. John's to celebrate Bishop Paul Moore's farewell to the diocese of New York. The lessons were read in English, Spanish, and French. St. Augustine's Gospel Choir sang; so did the choristers of the Cathedral School; and so did James Taylor. A black city councilman, a councilwoman, the president of Yale, and a fellow bishop spoke. They praised and thanked a man who is the embodiment of what this country can be, a person of Brahmin features and heritage who became a spokesman for the poor and powerless, who opened the church to them, and who embraced the women, the minorities, the homosexuals.

That afternoon Bishop Moore gave his final charge to the diocese and concluded.

You are messengers clothed in the beauty of God. Take hope, be strong, be brave, be free, be open, be loving, and hold up the vision of the Heavenly City. Remove the scales from your eyes, so that you can see the City so clearly that you will never cease until you have built Jerusalem in our land.[55]

And when the service seemed to have ended, he started down the nave of the cathedral, singing out as in a litany the names of all the parishes in the diocese, stopping, rocking on his heels, interspersing anecdotes, pausing to acknowledge friends. He held the congregation in his song, and the people of God embraced him in turn.

NOTES

Chapter One

1. Charles Murray, *Losing Ground: American Social Policy, 1950–1980* (New York: Basic Books, 1984), and Thomas Sowell, *A Conflict of Visions* (New York: Morrow, 1987). These sentiments go back, of course, to Edmund Burke's 1790 *Reflections on the Revolution in France*.

2. See Richard John Neuhaus, *The Naked Public Square: Religion and Democracy in America* (Grand Rapids, Mich.: W. B. Eerdmans, 1984); John P. Diggins, *The Lost Soul of American Politics: Virtue, Self-Interest, and the Foundations of Liberalism* (New York: Basic Books, 1984); Michael J. Sandel, "The Procedural Republic and the Unencumbered Self," *Political Theory* 12 (1984): 81–96; Robert N. Bellah et al., *Habits of the Heart: Individualism and Commitment in American Life* (Berkeley and Los Angeles: University of California Press, 1985); Christopher Lasch, *The Culture of Narcissism: American Life in an Age of Diminishing Expectations* (New York: Warner Books, 1979); and Philip Slater, *The Pursuit of Loneliness: American Culture at the Breaking Point* (Boston: Beacon Press, 1970).

3. Jürgen Habermas, *The Theory of Communicative Action*, trans. Thomas McCarthy, 2 vols. (Boston: Beacon Press, 1985–87), and Benjamin R. Barber, *Strong Democracy: Participatory Politics for a New Age* (Berkeley and Los Angeles: University of California Press, 1984).

4. For a similar, historically more comprehensive schema, see Carl Mitcham, "In Search of a New Relation between Science, Technology, and Society," *Technology in Society* 11 (1989): 409–17, and "Three Ways of Being-With Technology," in *From Artifact to Habitat: Studies in the Critical Engagement of Technology*, ed. Gayle L. Ormiston (Bethlehem, Pa.: Lehigh University Press, 1990), 31–59.

5. Henri-Georges Clouzot, *The Mystery of Picasso*, France, 1955; color, 85 min.

6. For a recent picture of our foreign debt, see Peter Passell, "America's Position in the Economic Race," *New York Times*, 4 Mar. 1990, sec. 4, 4–5.

7. Benjamin M. Friedman, "The Campaign's Hidden Issues," *New York Review of Books*, 13 Oct. 1988, 37.

8. Curtis B. Gans, "Is TV Turning Off the American Voter?" *New York Times*, 7 Mar. 1988, sec. 4, 24 and 28. See also Frances Fox Piven and Richard A. Cloward, *Why Americans Don't Vote* (New York: Pantheon, 1989).

9. In 1986, 87 percent of all U.S. citizens over eighteen were licensed to drive. See *Statistical Abstract of the United States 1990* (Washington, D.C.: U.S. Department of Commerce, 1990), 13 and 608. In 1990, 96 percent of all homes had color television. See Jon Van, "T.V.'s Impact on Society Not Slowing," *Chicago Tribune*, 3 June 1990, sec. 7, 1.

10. "Voter Turnout Shows Decline in 48 States," *Missoulian*, 14 Nov. 1988, 10.

11. Thomas Ferguson and Joel Rogers, "The Myth of America's Turn to the Right," *Atlantic*, May 1986, 43–53, and "Pocketbook Voting," *Scientific American*, July 1986, 62.

12. Robert Heilbroner, "The Triumph of Capitalism," *New Yorker*, 23 Jan. 1989, 107–8.

13. Christopher Jencks, "Deadly Neighborhoods," *New Republic*, 13 June 1988, 23–32.

14. Michael Fumento, "The Political Uses of an Epidemic," *New Republic*, 8/15 Aug. 1988, 19–23.

15. Ethan A. Nadelmann, "The Case for Legalization," *Public Interest* no. 92 (Summer 1988): 24, 14.

16. John Horgan, "Ignorance in Action," *Scientific American*, Nov. 1988, 17.

17. Lester C. Thurow, "US Drug Policy: Colossal Ignorance," *New York Times*, 8 May 1988, sec. 4, 29.

18. Michael Isikoff, "'Two-Tier' Drug Culture Seen Emerging," *Washington Post*, 3 Jan. 1989, A3.

19. Barbara Kantrowitz, "Three's a Crowd," *Newsweek*, 1 Sept. 1986, 68–76, and Martha Smilgis, "Here Come the DINKs," *Time*, 20 Apr. 1987, 75.

20. Lawrence M. Friedman, *Total Justice* (New York: Russell Sage Foundation, 1985), 43, 60.

21. Ibid., 154.

22. "Sorry, Your Policy Is Cancelled," *Time*, 24 Mar. 1986, 16–26.

23. Christine Sistare, "On the Use of Strict Liability in the Criminal Law," *Canadian Journal of Philosophy* 17 (1987): 395–407.

24. Jeffrey O'Connell and Rita James Simon, "Payment for Pain and Suffering: Who Wants What, When and Why?" *University of Illinois Law Forum* (1972): 1–55, and O'Connell and Theodore M. Bailey, "The History of Payment for Pain and Suffering," *University of Illinois Law Forum* (1972): 83–109.

25. Friedman, *Total Justice*, 154, and O'Connell and Simon, "Payment for Pain and Suffering," 1–2, 5.

26. O'Connell and Simon, "Payment for Pain and Suffering," 26–27.

27. Alex C. Michalos, "Optimism in Thirty Countries over a Decade," *Social Indicators Research* 20 (1988): 177–80.

28. Adrian Lyons, "The United States Revisited"; John F. X. Harriot, "American Foreign Policy: A European Perspective"; David Elly, "A Note from Across the Border"; and Jean-Yves Calvez, "The United States and the U.S. Church," *America* 158 (7 May 1988): 470–84.

29. American Agenda, Inc., Gerald R. Ford and Jimmy Carter, Chairmen, *American Agenda: Report to the Forty-First President of the United States of America* (Camp Hill, Pa.: Book-of-the-Month Club, n.d.); Benjamin M. Friedman, "In an Economic Fix," *New York Review of Books*, 22 Dec. 1988, 18–19; U.S. Congress, Office of Technology Assessment, *Technology and the American Economic Transition: Choices for the Future* (Washington, D.C.: U.S. Government Printing Office, 1988), 15–54, 443–63; Suzanne Berger et al., "Toward a New Industrial America," *Scientific American*, June 1989, 39–47; and George C. Lodge, "It's Time for an American Perestroika," *Atlantic*, Apr. 1989, 35–36.

30. *Webster's Ninth New Collegiate Dictionary*, s.v. "hyperactive."

31. Stephen W. Porges and Karen M. Smith, "Defining Hyperactivity: Psychophysiological and Behavioral Strategies," in *Hyperactive Children*, ed. Carol K. Whalen and Barbara Henker (New York: Academic Press, 1980), 75–104, and A. J. Zametkin et al., "Cerebral Glucose Metabolism in Adults with Hyperactivity of Childhood Onset," *New England Journal of Medicine* 323 (15 Nov. 1990): 1361–66.

32. Stephen Labaton, "The Trials and Errors of Boyd Jefferies," *New York Times*, 15 Jan. 1989, sec. 3, 1 and 10.

33. Lawrence Shames, "A Greed for Work," *New York Times Magazine*, 4 Dec. 1988, sec. 2, 30, and James Horley, Barbara Carroll, and Brian R. Little, "A Typology of Lifestyles," *Social Indicators Research* 20 (1988): 383–98.

For evidence that the amount of work and the amount of power are correlated, see also Frank P. Stafford and Greg J. Duncan, "The Use of Time and Technology by Households in the United States," in *Time, Goods, and Well-Being*, ed. F. Thomas Juster and Stafford (Ann Arbor, Mich.: Survey Research Center, University of Michigan, 1985), 253, 257, 270, 271, and John P. Robinson, "Changes in Time Use: An Historical Overview," ibid., 308 and 309.

34. Mike Parker and Jane Slaughter, "Management by Stress," *Technology Review*, Oct. 1988, 37–44.

35. U.S. Congress, Office of Technology Assessment, *Technology and the American Economic Transition*, 382–83.

36. Bellah, "Resurrecting the Common Good," *Commonweal* 114 (18 Dec. 1987): 740. See also James Fallows, "The Hard Life," *Atlantic*, Mar. 1989, 16–26.

37. Ronald Dworkin, "The New England," *New York Review of Books*, 27 Oct. 1988, 58.

Chapter Two

1. Daniel Bell, *The Coming of Post-Industrial Society: A Venture in Social Forecasting* (New York: Basic Books, [1973] 1976), 53–54.

2. Ibid., 34–36.

3. Ernst Robert Curtius, *European Literature and the Latin Middle Ages*, trans. Willard R. Trask (London: Routledge, 1953), 251–54, and Jürgen Habermas, "Modernity versus Postmodernity," *New German Critique* no. 22 (Winter 1981): 3.

4. Curtius, *European Literature*, 20.

5. Habermas, "Modernity versus Postmodernity," 3–4.

6. Curtius, *European Literature*, 20–24.

7. Martin Luther, "Von der Freiheit eines Christenmenschen," *Ausgewählte Schriften*, ed. Karin Bornkamm and Gerhard Ebeling, 6 vols. (Frankfurt: Insel, 1982) 1:238–63.

8. John Donne, *The Anniversaries*, ed. Frank Manley (Baltimore: Johns Hopkins University Press, 1963), 73–74. For the wider setting of this passage, see Stephen Toulmin, *Cosmopolis: The Hidden Agenda of Modernity* (New York: Free Press, 1990), 62–69.

9. "Modernism," as a glance at the *Oxford English Dictionary* will show, has been used in many senses. For example, it has been used to designate an aesthetic movement that began in the early twentieth century. To make that sense its exclusive meaning, however, as Daniel Joseph Singal urges, seems

ahistorical and dogmatic. See Singal, "Towards a Definition of American Modernism," *American Quarterly* 39 (1987): 7–8.

10. René Descartes, *Discourse on Method*, trans. Laurence J. Lafleur (Indianapolis: Bobbs-Merrill, 1956); Francis Bacon, *The Great Instauration and New Atlantis*, ed. J. Weinberger (Arlington Heights, Ill.: Harlan Davidson, 1980); and John Locke, *Treatise of Civil Government and a Letter Concerning Toleration*, ed. Charles L. Sherman (New York: Appleton-Century-Crofts, 1965).

11. Elizabeth Alvilda Petroff, "Introduction," in *Medieval Women's Visionary Literature*, ed. Petroff (New York: Oxford University Press, 1986), 37–44.

12. This is to see Bacon's, Descartes's, and Locke's relation to Christianity schematically and retrospectively. For a more detailed and nuanced account, see Charles Taylor, *Sources of the Self: The Making of the Modern Identity* (Cambridge, Mass.: Harvard University Press, 1989), 139–42, 230–33, 234–47.

13. William Leiss, *The Domination of Nature* (New York: George Braziller, 1972), 57–61.

14. Bacon, *The Great Instauration and New Atlantis*, 2; Descartes, *Meditations*, trans. Lafleur (Indianapolis: Bobbs-Merrill, 1960), 17; and Locke, *Treatise of Civil Government*, 4.

15. For the story of how the self detached itself from the world while continuing to draw on sources beyond itself, see Taylor, *Sources of the Self*.

16. *The Portable Thomas Jefferson*, ed. Merrill D. Peterson (Harmondsworth: Penguin, 1977), 435–36.

17. Habermas, "Die Moderne—ein unvollendetes Projekt," *Kleine politische Schriften* (Frankfurt: Suhrkamp, 1981), 444–64.

18. Alfred D. Chandler, Jr., *The Visible Hand: The Managerial Revolution in American Business* (Cambridge, Mass.: Harvard University Press, 1977), 84.

19. For the power of dynamite, see Bryan Di Salvatore, "Dynamite," *New Yorker*, 27 Apr. 1987, 42–72, and 4 May 1987, 38–58.

20. John F. Stover, *American Railroads* (Chicago: University of Chicago Press, 1961), 11, 224.

21. William Wordsworth, *Poetical Works*, 2d ed., ed. E. de Selincourt and Helen Darbshire (Oxford: Clarendon Press, 1954), 61–62. See also Leo Marx, *The Machine in the Garden* (London: Oxford University Press, 1964), 3–33.

22. *Workin' on the Railroad*, ed. Richard Reinhardt (Palo Alto, Calif.: American West, 1970), 57–58.

23. "Flathead Railroad Treaty, 1882," in *The Last Best Place*, ed. William Kittredge and Annick Smith (Helena, Mont.: Montana, 1988), 359.

24. Ibid., 354, 358.

25. Ibid., 358, 363. What the Native Americans gave and what they kept in the Hellgate Treaty of 1855 is still in dispute. See Ron Selden, "Landowners, Irrigators Weigh in against Tribes," *Missoulian*, 31 Oct. 1990, B2.

26. "Flathead Railroad Treaty," 357–58, and Eugene V. Smalley, *History of the Northern Pacific Railroad* (New York: Putnam, 1883), 420.

27. Smalley, *History of the Northern Pacific Railroad*, 416.

28. Ibid., 417–18.

29. Ibid., 416.

30. Louis Tuck Renz, *The History of the Northern Pacific Railroad* (Fairfield, Wash.: Galleon, 1980), 96.

31. *Workin' on the Railroad*, 70.

32. Ibid., 72, 74–75, 77–81.

33. Ibid., 76–77.

34. Smalley, *History of the Northern Pacific Railroad*, 419.

35. Leonora Koelbel, *Missoula the Way It Was* (Missoula, Mont.: Gateway, 1972), 57.

36. Stover, *American Railroads*, 74–76.

37. Chandler, *The Visible Hand*, 145–87.

38. Stover, *American Railroads*, 4 and 10, and Chandler, *The Visible Hand*, 87.

39. Ralph Waldo Emerson, "The Young American," *Essays and Lectures*, ed. Joel Porte (New York: Library of America, 1983), 216, 213.

40. Marx, *The Machine in the Garden*, 196–202.

41. *Workin' on the Railroad*, 219, 220, 221. See also Emerson, "The Young American," 215.

42. *Workin' on the Railroad*, 223.

43. Henry G. Bugbee, "Wilderness in America," *Journal of the American Academy of Religion* 42 (1974): 614–15.

44. Wallace Stegner, *Angle of Repose* (New York: Fawcett, 1972), 344.

45. Sherry Devlin, "A Water Supply at Risk," *Missoulian*, 8 Oct. 1989, F1–F2, and "Search for BN Contaminants Goes Full Bore," *Missoulian*, 1 Nov. 1989, B1.

46. Eugene S. Ferguson, "The Steam Engine before 1830," in *Technology in Western Civilization*, ed. Melvin Kranzberg and Carroll W. Pursell, Jr., 2 vols. (New York: Oxford University Press, 1967), 1:245–63; John B. Rae, "The Invention of Invention," ibid., 1:334–35; and Rae, "Energy Conversion," ibid., 1:339–43.

47. Chandler, *The Visible Hand*, 147, 153, 158–59, and Michael J. Piore and Charles F. Sabel, *The Second Industrial Divide: Possibilities for Prosperity* (New York: Basic Books, 1984), 50–65. Bureaucracy is sometimes an aspect and at other times a variant of the corporation. See Max Weber, *Economy and Society: An Outline of Interpretive Sociology*, trans. Ephraim Fischoff et al., ed. Guenther Roth and Claus Wittich (New York: Bedminster Press, 1968), 974. On bureaucracy as a response to complexity, see Weber, *Economy and Society*, 972. On the rational character of bureaucracy and corporation, see Weber, *Economy and Society*, 987–89, 1002, and Chandler, *The Visible Hand*, 95.

48. Chandler, *The Visible Hand*, 179, 201, and Piore and Sabel, *The Second Industrial Divide*, 68–69.

49. Descartes, *Discourse on Method*, 12.

50. On the organic holism and limitations of the precorporate and prebureaucratic economy, see Weber, *Economy and Society* 956–57, and Chandler, *The Visible Hand*, 18, 35–36, 47.

51. Weber, *Economy and Society*, 975, and Chandler, *The Visible Hand*, 108.

52. Descartes, *Discourse on Method*, 12–14.

53. Piore and Sabel, *The Second Industrial Divide*, 64.

54. Weber, *Economy and Society*, 973–75.

55. John Kenneth Galbraith, *Economics and the Public Purpose* (Boston: Houghton Mifflin, 1973), 81–154.

56. Stover, *American Railroads*, 157–58. Scientific concerns, however,

not economic ones, gave the initial impulse to the establishment of standard time. See Ian R. Bartky, "The Adoption of Standard Time," *Technology and Culture* 30 (1989): 25–56.

57. Chandler, *The Visible Hand*, 36–37.

58. Piore and Sabel, *The Second Industrial Divide*, 29–35.

59. Chandler, *The Visible Hand*, 137–44.

60. Ibid., 94–109.

61. Weber, *Economy and Society*, 958–59, 962, 968; Galbraith, *The New Industrial State*, 2d ed. (Boston: Houghton Mifflin, 1972), 128–58; and Chandler, *The Visible Hand*, 3–4, 95, 180–81.

62. Galbraith, *Economics and the Public Purpose*, 42–44, and Piore and Sabel, *The Second Industrial Divide*, 50.

63. Piore and Sabel, *The Second Industrial Divide*, 19–48.

64. John C. Coates IV, "State Takeover Statutes and Corporate Theory: The Revival of an Old Debate," *New York University Law Review* 64 (1989): 806–76.

65. Locke, *Treatise of Civil Government*, 5–12, 20, 21, and passim.

66. Alexis de Tocqueville, *Democracy in America*, ed. Phillips Bradley, 2 vols. (New York: Vintage, 1945), 2:104.

67. Locke, *Treatise of Civil Government*, 18–33.

68. Josiah Royce, "The Pacific Coast," *Race Questions, Provincialism and Other American Problems* (New York: Macmillan, 1908), 169, 173.

69. Henry Sumner Maine, *Ancient Law: Its Connection with the Early History of Society and Its Relation to Modern Ideas* (London: J. Murray, 1912), 123–74; Hannah Arendt, *The Human Condition* (Chicago: University of Chicago Press, 1958), 50–67; and Jean Bethke Elshtain, *Public Man, Private Woman: Women in Social and Political Thought* (Princeton, N.J.: Princeton University Press, 1981), 3–16.

70. For the description and discussion of such a festive occasion, see *Abbot Suger on the Abbey Church of St.-Denis and Its Art Treasures*, trans. and ed. Erwin Panofsky, 2d ed. by Gerda Panofsky-Soergel (Princeton, N.J.: Princeton University Press, 1979), and Otto von Simson, *The Gothic Cathedral*, 2d ed. (Princeton, N.J.: Princeton University Press, 1962), 129–41.

71. Richard Sennett, *The Fall of Public Man: The Forces Eroding Public Life and Burdening the Modern Psyche with Roles It Cannot Perform* (New York: Knopf, 1977), 45–122.

72. Ibid., 123–255.

73. John R. Stilgoe, *Metropolitan Corridor: Railroads and the American Scene* (New Haven, Conn.: Yale University Press, 1983), 36–45.

74. Ibid., 189–221.

75. Ibid., 335–45.

76. Ada Louise Huxtable, "Creeping Gigantism in Manhattan," *New York Times*, 22 Mar. 1987, sec. 2, 1 and 36.

77. Thomas Huff, "Thinking Clearly about Privacy," *Washington Law Review* 55 (1980): 785–86, and Judith W. Decew, "Defending the 'Private' in Constitutional Privacy," *Journal of Value Inquiry* 21 (1987): 171–84.

78. Huff, "Thinking Clearly about Privacy," 779, 786.

79. Ibid., 777–94.

80. Ibid., 780.

81. *I'll Buy That!: Fifty Small Wonders and Big Deals that Revolu-*

tionized the Lives of Consumers (Mount Vernon, N.Y.: Consumer Reports Books, 1986), xii.

82. F. Thomas Juster, "Investments of Time by Men and Women," in *Time, Goods, and Well-Being,* ed. Juster and Frank P. Stafford (Ann Arbor, Mich.: Survey Research Center, University of Michigan, 1985), 173, and Juster, "A Note on Recent Changes in Time Use," ibid., 317.

83. Juster, "Investments of Time," 173.

84. Martha S. Hill, "Patterns of Time Use," in *Time, Goods, and Well-Being,* 135–37.

85. Stafford and Greg J. Duncan, "The Use of Time and Technology by Households in the United States," in *Time, Goods, and Well-Being,* 271, 274, and John P. Robinson, "Changes in Time Use: An Historical Overview," ibid., 309, 311.

86. Hill, "Patterns of Time Use," 138. As Robert Kubey and Mihaly Csikszentmihalyi point out in *Television and the Quality of Life: How Viewing Shapes Everyday Experience* (Hillsdale, N.J.: L. Erlbaum Associates, 1990), watching television with family members, the usual setting, is more pleasant than watching alone (73–74, 111). But personal interaction is more vigorous without television (116–17).

87. Juster, "Investments of Time," 173.

88. Tocqueville, *Democracy in America,* 2:106.

89. Juster, "Preferences for Work and Leisure," in *Time, Goods, and Well-Being,* 337, 336; Greg K. Dow and Juster, "Goods, Time, and Well-Being: The Joint Dependence Problem," ibid., 404; and Kubey and Csikszentmihalyi, *Television and the Quality of Life,* 80–87, 164, 172–73.

90. Robinson, "Changes in Time Use," 309–10.

91. Juster, "A Note on Recent Changes in Time Use," 315, 317, 319.

92. Stafford and Duncan, "The Use of Time and Technology," 270, and Juster, "Preferences for Work and Leisure," 340–44.

93. Locke, *Treatise of Civil Government,* 19, 22–23, 32; see also p. 27.

94. Ibid., 20, 27.

95. Piore and Sabel, *The Second Industrial Divide,* 66–67.

96. Galbraith, *The New Industrial State* (Boston: Houghton Mifflin, 1967).

Chapter Three

1. Others have done it well, notably Jean-François Lyotard, *The Postmodern Condition,* trans. Geoff Bennington and Brian Massumi, Theory and History of Literature, vol. 10 (Minneapolis: University of Minnesota Press, 1984); Charles Jencks, *Post-Modernism* (New York, Rizzoli, 1987); Wolfgang Welsch, "Vielheit ohne Einheit?" *Philosophisches Jahrbuch* 94 (1987): 111–41; and David Harvey, *The Condition of Postmodernity: An Enquiry into the Origins of Cultural Change* (Oxford: Blackwell, 1990). I should note that Harvey has preceded my effort to link postmodern intellectual, cultural, and economic developments. His survey of the literature is much more comprehensive than mine, and his orientation and conclusion are quite different from mine.

2. See Richard Rorty, *Philosophy and the Mirror of Nature* (Princeton, N.J.: Princeton University Press, 1979), 162 and 317 on the weakness of this claim.

3. See ibid.

4. See Stephen Toulmin, *Cosmopolis: The Hidden Agenda of Modernity* (New York: Free Press, 1990), 45–87.

5. Rorty, *Philosophy and the Mirror of Nature*, 389.

6. Like all writers of our generation, Rorty had to learn how to go from gender-biased to gender-neutral language. In *Philosophy and the Mirror of Nature* he tried the awkward transitional device of asking the reader to understand that terms "such as 'himself' and 'men' should, throughout this book, be taken as abbreviations for 'himself or herself,' 'men and women,' and so on" (4, n. 1).

7. Ibid., 347, 300. Catherine Z. Elgin similarly asserts that "things do not present themselves to us in any privileged vocabulary or system of categories" (Nelson Goodman and Elgin, *Reconceptions in Philosophy and Other Arts and Sciences* [Indianapolis: Hackett, 1988], 7).

8. *Machina ex Dea: Feminist Perspectives on Technology*, ed. Joan Rothschild (New York: Pergamon Press, 1983).

9. Carolyn Merchant, "Mining the Earth's Womb," ibid., 99–117.

10. Rothschild, "Technology, Housework, and Women's Liberation: A Theoretical Analysis," ibid., 79–93, and Corlann Gee Bush, "Women and the Assessment of Technology: To Think, to Be; to Unthink, to Free," ibid., 151–69.

11. René Descartes, *Discourse on Method*, trans. Laurence J. Lafleur (Indianapolis: Bobbs-Merrill, 1956), 15–20.

12. Immanuel Kant, *Foundations of the Metaphysics of Morals*, trans. Lewis White Beck (Indianapolis: Bobbs-Merrill, 1959).

13. Ibid., 39.

14. Georg Wilhelm Friedrich Hegel, *Philosophy of Right*, trans. T. M. Knox (London: Oxford University Press, 1952), 28, 33, 89–90.

15. Lawrence Kohlberg, *The Philosophy of Moral Development: Moral Stages and the Idea of Justice* (New York: Harper & Row, 1981), 412.

16. Kohlberg, Charles Levine, and Alexandra Hewer, *Moral Stages: A Current Formulation and a Response to Critics* (Basel: Karger, 1983).

17. Carol Gilligan, *In a Different Voice: Psychological Theory and Women's Development* (Cambridge, Mass.: Harvard University Press, 1982), 18.

18. Kohlberg, *The Philosophy of Moral Development*, 410.

19. Gilligan, *In a Different Voice*, 25–32.

20. Michael Walzer, *Spheres of Justice: A Defense of Pluralism and Equality* (New York: Basic Books, 1983), 10–13.

21. Philip J. Davis and Reuben Hersh, *Descartes' Dream: The World According to Mathematics* (San Diego: Harcourt Brace Jovanovich, 1986); Thomas S. Kuhn, *The Structure of Scientific Revolutions* (Chicago: University of Chicago Press, 1962); Stephen Jay Gould, *Wonderful Life: The Burgess Shale and the Nature of History* (New York: W. W. Norton, 1989); Clifford Geertz, *Local Knowledge: Further Essays in Interpretive Anthropology* (New York: Basic Books, 1983); Suzanna Sherry, "Civic Virtue and the Feminine Voice in Constitutional Adjudication," *Virginia Law Review* 72 (1986): 543–616; and Jacques Derrida, *Writing and Difference*, trans. Alan Bass (Chicago: University of Chicago Press, 1978).

22. Louise Erdrich, *Love Medicine* (Toronto: Bantam, 1984).

23. Ibid., 6.

24. Robert N. Bellah et al., *Habits of the Heart* (Berkeley and Los Angeles: University of California Press, 1985), 53–141.

25. Ibid., 55–56, 144–47.

26. Ibid., 152–62.

27. Jane Jacobs, *The Death and Life of Great American Cities* (New York: Vintage, 1961), 7, 23, 338–71, and Vincent Scully, *American Architecture and Urbanism*, rev. ed. (New York: H. Holt, 1988), 280–81.

28. Jacobs, *The Death and Life of Great American Cities*, 20, 177, and Scully, *American Architecture and Urbanism*, 167, 251.

29. Jacobs, *The Death and Life of Great American Cities*, 3–25; Jencks, *Post-Modernism*, 27, 29; and Scully, *American Architecture and Urbanism* 164–66, 171, 173, 180, 198, 241–42, 245–49.

30. Jacobs, *The Death and Life of Great American Cities*, 23, 418, 435–40; Jencks, *Post-Modernism*, 29; and Scully, *American Architecture and Urbanism*, 184, 190–92.

31. Jencks, *Post-Modernism*, 29, and Scully, *American Architecture and Urbanism*, 178.

32. Kent C. Bloomer and Charles W. Moore, *Body, Memory and Architecture* (New Haven, Conn.: Yale University Press, 1977), 1, 73–74.

33. Scully, *American Architecture and Urbanism*, 169, 193, 252, 291.

34. Ibid., 167–69.

35. Paul Goldberger, "Why Design Can't Transform Cities," *New York Times*, 25 June 1989, sec. 2, 1 and 30.

36. Scully, *American Architecture and Urbanism*, 142, 180, and Goldberger, "A Commission that Has Itself Become a Landmark," *New York Times*, 15 Apr. 1990, sec. 2, 36 and 40.

37. Scully, *American Architecture and Urbanism*, 257.

38. Ibid., 274–76.

39. Jencks, *Post-Modernism*, 250, 258, 272, 285, 297, 315, 346–50, and Scully, *American Architecture and Urbanism*, 195.

40. Daniel Bell, *The Coming of Post-Industrial Society: A Venture in Social Forecasting* (New York: Basic Books, 1976), xii, 26, 116, 126–27. See also U.S. Congress, Office of Technology Assessment, *Technology and the American Economic Transition: Choices for the Future* (Washington, D.C.: U.S. Government Printing Office, 1988), 151–58.

41. Eric D. Larson, Marc H. Ross, and Robert H. Williams, "Beyond the Era of Materials," *Scientific American*, June 1986, 34–41.

42. Bell, *The Coming of Post-Industrial Society*, 26.

43. John Kenneth Galbraith, *The New Industrial State*, 2d ed. (Boston: Houghton Mifflin, 1972), 45–71.

44. Christoph Lauterburg, *Vor dem Ende der Hierarchie*, 2d ed. (Düsseldorf: Econ, 1980), and U.S. Congress, Office of Technology Assessment, *Technology and the American Economic Transition*, 177–90.

45. John P. Robinson, "Changes in Time Use: An Historical Overview," in *Time, Goods, and Well-Being*, ed. F. Thomas Juster and Frank B. Stafford (Ann Arbor, Mich.: Survey Research Center, University of Michigan, 1985), 311.

46. See, for example, Peter Schmeisser, "Is America in Decline?" *New York Times Magazine*, 17 Apr. 1988, 24–27, 66–68, 96, and Paul Kennedy, "Can the U.S. Remain Number One?" *New York Review of Books*, 16 Mar. 1989, 36–42.

47. For the remainder of this section I draw in part on materials and obser-

vations in Michael J. Piore and Charles F. Sabel, *The Second Industrial Divide: Possibilities for Prosperity* (New York: Basic Books, 1984), 165–220.

48. Bell, *The Cultural Contradictions of Capitalism* (New York: Basic Books, 1976).

49. Piore and Sabel, *The Second Industrial Divide*, 184–87, and James Brian Quinn, Jordan J. Baruch, and Penny Cushman Paquette, "Technology in Services," *Scientific American*, Dec. 1987, 50–51.

50. Economic totalitarianism would not be the same as political totalitarianism. The former, unlike the latter, would have the consent and cooperation of the people as the giant corporations once did, thus leading to prosperity as the latter could not. Economic totalitarianism would come into being if people strongly preferred predictability to variety, security to independence, solidity to flexibility, and hard to soft solutions. But no such preference is emerging. On people's erstwhile allegiance to corporations, see Galbraith, *The New Industrial State*, 130–39.

51. Peter Passell, "America's Position in the Economic Race: What the Numbers Show and Conceal," *New York Times*, 4 Mar. 1990, sec. 4, 4–5.

52. Fred Block, "Postindustrial Development and the Obsolescence of Economic Categories," *Revising State Theory: Essays in Politics and Postindustrialism* (Philadelphia: Temple University Press, 1987), 142–70, and Jonathan Schlefer, "Making Sense of the Productivity Debate," *Technology Review*, Aug.–Sept. 1988, 28–40.

53. U.S. Congress, Office of Technology Assessment, *Technology and the American Economic Transition*, 462.

54. Denise Schmandt-Besserat, "The Earliest Precursor of Writing," in *The Emergence of Language: Development and Evolution*, ed. William S.-Y. Wang (New York: W. H. Freeman, 1989), 31–45. See also my "Texts and Things: Holding on to Reality," in *Lifeworld and Technology*, ed. Timothy Casey and Lester Embree (Washington, D.C.: University Press of America, 1989), 93–116.

55. Hubert L. Dreyfus and Stuart E. Dreyfus, *Mind over Machine: The Power of Human Intuition and Expertise in the Era of the Computer* (New York: Free Press, 1986); David F. Noble, *Forces of Production: Social History of Industrial Automation* (New York: Oxford University Press, 1986); and Walter W. Powell, "Explaining Technological Change," *American Journal of Sociology* 93 (1987): 185–97.

56. Shoshana Zuboff, *In the Age of the Smart Machine: The Future of Work and Power* (New York: Basic Books, 1988).

57. Ibid., 58–76, 80–96, 126–71, 207–15, 327–37, and James Rule and Paul Attewell, "What Do Computers Do?" *Social Problems* 36 (1989): 225–41.

58. Rule and Attewell, "What Do Computers Do?" 236–37.

59. Quinn et al., "Technology in Services," 57, and Elizabeth Corcoran, "Milliken and Co.: Managing the Quality of a Textile Revolution," *Scientific American*, Apr. 1990, 74 and 76.

60. Karen Wright, "The Shape of Things to Go," *Scientific American*, May 1990, 92–101.

61. National Research Council, *Alternative Agriculture* (Washington, D.C.: National Academy Press, 1989), 135–94.

62. David Gelernter, "The Metamorphosis of Information Management," *Scientific American*, Aug. 1989, 66.

63. Greg Lakes, "Typical Troubles, Exceptional Success," *Missoulian*, 8

Apr. 1990, F1, and "Sisters Find International Market for Their Wares," *Missoulian*, 8 Apr. 1990, F1.

64. "Stone Plans $15.5 Million Mill Project," *Missoulian*, 18 Nov. 1988, 1, and Jim Ludwick, "Stone Inaugurates Recycling Plant," *Missoulian*, 4 Nov. 1990, C1.

65. Piore and Sabel, *The Second Industrial Divide*, 213–20, and Martin T. Katzman, "From Horse Carts to Minimills," *Public Interest* no. 92 (1988): 121–35.

66. Piore and Sabel, *The Second Industrial Divide*, 28–35, 258–77. Related and competing paradigms are "the transformation scenario" in U.S. Congress, Office of Technology Assessment, *Technology and the American Economic Transition*, 87–141, 201–79, 425–41, and "lean production" in James P. Womack, Daniel T. Jones, and Daniel Roos, *The Machine that Changed the World* (New York: Rawson Associates, 1990).

67. Piore and Sabel, *The Second Industrial Divide*, 28–35.

68. Carol Kleiman, "Standards Stiffen in Financial Planning," *Chicago Tribune*, 30 Apr. 1989, sec. 8, 1. Investment newsletters constitute an alternative source of financial advice. They also produce more perplexity. Which of the more than one hundred newsletters should I trust? The *Hulbert Financial Digest* has the answer: it rates 120 investment letters. But can we trust Mark Hulbert? Never fear. A special committee has been formed to evaluate Hulbert's methods. By now we are at four or five removes from the tangible economy. See Stephen Advokat, "Newsletter Finds Its Niche Rating the Investment Newsletters," *Chicago Tribune*, 4 Nov. 1990, sec. 7, 12B.

69. Annetta Miller and Dody Tsiantar, "The Advice Peddlers," *Newsweek*, 22 May 1989, 60–61.

70. Bell, *The Coming of Post-Industrial Society*, 130–31, and Quinn et al., "Technology in Services," 50.

71. A more revealing ten-sector economy has been drawn up in U.S. Congress, Office of Technology Assessment, *Technology and the American Economic Transition*, 148–50.

72. Quinn et al., "Technology in Services," 56.

73. Piore and Sabel, *The Second Industrial Divide*, 19–48.

74. Daniel J. Boorstin, *Democracy and Its Discontents: Reflections on Everyday America* (New York: Vintage, 1975), 20–21.

75. Larry Hirschhorn, *Beyond Mechanization: Work and Technology in a Postindustrial Age* (Cambridge, Mass.: MIT Press, 1984)

76. Zuboff, *In the Age of the Smart Machine*, 197–99.

77. Ibid., 206–18, 362–86.

78. Suzanne Berger et al., "Toward a New Industrial America," *Scientific American*, June 1989, 41.

79. George C. Lodge, "It's Time for an American Perestroika," *Atlantic*, Apr. 1989, 35–36.

80. Bell, *The Coming of Post-Industrial Society*, 128, 159, 160 n. 30, 298, 364, 366, and Piore and Sabel, *The Second Industrial Divide*, 265–67, 269–70, 273–75, 279, 283, 303–6.

Chapter Four

1. Amory B. Lovins, "Energy Strategy: The Road Not Taken?" *Foreign Affairs* 55 (Oct. 1976): 65–96, esp. 77–78, 91–94.

2. Ralph Landau, "U.S. Economic Growth," *Scientific American*, June 1988, 44, 49, 52; Benjamin M. Friedman, "In an Economic Fix," *New York Review of Books*, 22 Dec. 1988, 18–19; and Suzanne Berger et al., "Toward a New Industrial America," *Scientific American*, June 1989, 46, 47.

3. See my *Technology and the Character of Contemporary Life: A Philosophical Inquiry* (Chicago: University of Chicago Press, 1984).

4. See ibid., 85–101.

5. Shoshana Zuboff, *In the Age of the Smart Machine: The Future of Work and Power* (New York: Basic Books, 1988), 63; see also xii, 59, 62.

6. Ibid., 85–95. See also U.S. Congress, Office of Technology Assessment, *Automation and the Workplace: Selected Labor, Education, and Training Issues* (Washington, D.C.: U.S. Government Printing Office, 1983).

7. Zuboff, *In the Age of the Smart Machine*, 90.

8. Umberto Eco, *Travels in Hyperreality: Essays*, trans. William Weaver (San Diego: Harcourt Brace Jovanovich, 1986), 3–58, and Jean Baudrillard, *Selected Writings*, ed. Mark Poster (Stanford, Calif.: Stanford University Press, 1988), 166–84.

9. Stewart Brand, *The Media Lab: Inventing the Future at MIT* (New York: Viking, 1987), 30.

10. Ronald F. E. Weissman, "From the Personal Computer to the Scholar's Workstation," *Academic Computing* 3 (Oct. 1988): 11, and Chris Raymond, "Humanities Researchers Experience a 'Sea Change' in the Use of Computers in Their Disciplines," *Chronicle of Higher Education*, 12 July 1989, A6–A8.

11. James R. Chiles, "When Pilots' Worst Nightmares Come True—In Simulators," *Smithsonian*, June 1986, 78–87, and Ralph Norman Haber, "Flight Simulation," *Scientific American*, July 1986, 96–103.

12. Haber, "Flight Simulation," 103.

13. Ibid., and Chiles, "When Pilots' Worst Nightmares Come True," 83–84.

14. Haber, "Flight Simulation," 103, and Brand, *The Media Lab*, 139.

15. Zuboff, *In the Age of the Smart Machine*, 58–96, 159–71, 327–37, 362–86.

16. Brand, *The Media Lab*, 90; Joseph Bronzino, Vincent H. Smith, and Maurice L. Wade, *Medical Technology and Society: An Interdisciplinary Perspective* (Cambridge, Mass.: MIT Press, 1990), 305–21, 369–508; and Edward H. Shortliffe, "Computer Programs to Support Clinical Decision Making," *Journal of the American Medical Association* 258 (3 July 1987): 61–66.

17. Jean Seligman and Linda Buckley, "A Sickroom with a View," *Newsweek*, 26 Mar. 1990, 61.

18. Quoted in Marion Long, "The Seers' Catalog," *Omni*, Jan. 1987, 38.

19. Quoted ibid., 40.

20. Woody Allen, "The Kugelmass Episode," *Side Effects* (New York: Ballantine, 1981), 61–62.

21. Ibid., 63–65.

22. Ibid., 77.

23. John P. Robinson, "Changes in Time Use: An Historical Overview," *Time, Goods, and Well-Being*, ed. F. Thomas Juster and Frank P. Stafford (Ann Arbor, Mich.: Survey Research Center, University of Michigan, 1985), 289–311, and Robert Kubey and Mihaly Csikszentmihalyi, *Television and the Quality of Life: How Viewing Shapes Everyday Experience* (Hillsdale, N.J.: L. Erlbaum Associates, 1990).

24. Jon Van, "TV's Impact on Society Not Slowing," *Chicago Tribune*, 3 June 1990, sec. 7, 1.

25. Hans Fantel, "New Projectors Put the Viewer in the Big Picture," *New York Times*, 28 Jan. 1990, sec. 2, 18.

26. Sherry Turkle, *The Second Self: Computers and the Human Spirit* (New York: Simon and Schuster, 1984), 64–92, and Kubey and Csikszentmihalyi, *Television and the Quality of Life*, 143–44.

27. For a survey of computer networks, see Rick Kirkham, "Computer Networks," *APA Newsletter* 89, no. 2 (Winter 1990): 34–39, and Karen Wright, "The Road to the Global Village," *Scientific American*, Mar. 1990, 83–94.

28. Justine de Lacy, "The Sexy Computer," *Atlantic*, July 1987, 18–26; Brand, *The Media Lab*, 25–26, and Hugh Kenner, "Out My Computer Window," *Harper's*, Nov. 1989, 76–80.

29. Maureen Dowd, "Eighty-Eightsomething," *New Republic*, 1 Aug. 1988, 37–40.

30. Tim Luke, "Televisual Democracy and the Politics of Charisma," *Telos* no. 70 (Winter 1986–87): 59–79, and Fred W. Friendly, "On Television: News, Lies and Videotape," *New York Times*, 6 Aug. 1989, sec. 2, 1 and 27.

31. Joshua Meyrowitz, *No Sense of Place: The Impact of Electronic Media on Social Behavior* (New York: Oxford University Press, 1985), 118–22.

32. Erik Larson, "Brave New Foods," *Harper's*, May 1988, 18–22, and James Gorman, "Nothing to Sink Your Teeth Into," *New York Times Magazine*, 11 June 1989, 40, 42, 44.

33. Bill Bard, "Climb Every Mountain, Before Lunch," *Newsweek*, 13 Nov. 1989, 102.

34. Charles Leerhsen, "How Disney Does It," *Newsweek*, 3 Apr. 1989, 50.

35. Ibid., 49.

36. Gorman, "Nothing to Sink Your Teeth Into," 42.

37. Ibid., 42.

38. Ellen K. Coughlin, "Is Violence on TV Harmful to Our Health?" *Chronicle of Higher Education*, 13 Mar. 1985, 5 and 8.

39. Arguments can be found in my "Artificial Realities," in *The Presence of Feeling in Thought*, ed. Bernard Den Ouden and Marcia Moen (New York: Peter Lang, 1992).

40. This is most evident in the case of televised hyperreality. See Kubey and Csikszentmihalyi, *Television and the Quality of Life*, 119–48, 186–87.

41. Ibid., 130, 133 34, 137.

42. William J. Donelly, *The Confetti Generation* (New York: H. Holt, 1983), 173–98.

43. Allen, "The Kugelmass Episode," 78.

44. Hildegard of Bingen, *Scivias*, bk. 3, vision 13, in *Opera Omnia*, ed. F. A. Reuss and J. P. Migne, *Patrologia Latina* (Paris, 1882), v. 197, col. 732; my translation. "God's Grandeur" is in Gerald Manley Hopkins, *Poems and Prose*, ed. W. H. Gardner (Harmondsworth: Penguin, 1953), 27.

45. Karl Marx and Friedrich Engels, *The Communist Manifesto*, ed. Samuel H. Beer (New York: Appleton-Century-Crofts, 1955), 13.

46. Ernst Jünger, "Die totale Mobilmachung," *Werke*, 10 vols. (Stuttgart: Klett, [1960–61]), 5:123–47.

47. On the amalgams of conservatism and technocracy Germany produced between the World Wars, see Jeffrey Herf, *Reactionary Modernism: Technol-*

ogy, Culture, and Politics in Weimar and the Third Reich (Cambridge: Cambridge University Press, 1984).

48. C. David Jenkins, "Psychologic and Social Precursors of Coronary Disease," New England Journal of Medicine 284 (4 Feb. 1971): 244.

49. Meyer Friedman and Ray H. Rosenman, "Association of Specific Overt Behavior Pattern with Blood and Cardiovascular Findings," Journal of the American Medical Association 169 (21 Mar. 1959): 1286.

50. Jenkins, "Psychologic and Social Precursors of Coronary Disease," 309. See also Rosenman et al., "A Predictive Study of Coronary Heart Disease," Journal of the American Medical Association 189 (6 July 1964): 15–22, and Jenkins, "The Coronary-Prone Personality," in Psychological Aspects of Myocardial Infarction and Coronary Care, ed. W. Doyle Gentry and Redford B. Williams, Jr. (Saint Louis: Mosby, 1975), 5–23.

51. Bronzino et al., Medical Technology and Society, 42, and James Horley, Barbara Carroll, and Brian R. Little, "A Typology of Lifestyles," Social Indicators Research 20 (1988): 389.

52. Peter T. Kilborn, "Tales from the Digital Treadmill," New York Times, 3 June 1990, sec. 4, 1 and 3.

53. Nancy Gibbs, "How America Has Run Out of Time," Time, 24 Apr. 1989, 60.

54. Stephen Labaton, "The Trials and Errors of Boyd Jefferies," New York Times, 15 Jan. 1989, sec. 3, 1 and 10.

55. Staffan B. Linder, The Harried Leisure Class (New York: Columbia University Press, 1970).

56. Dante Alighieri, The Inferno, trans. John Ciardi (New York: New American Library, 1954), 76.

57. Explorations in Communication, ed. Edmund Carpenter and Marshall McLuhan (Boston: Beacon Press, 1960), xi. See also Daniel Bell, The Coming of Post-Industrial Society: A Venture in Social Forecasting (New York: Basic Books, 1976), 128, 129, 160 n. 30, 298, 364, 366.

58. Bell, The Coming of Post-Industrial Society, xv.

59. Gary Stix, "Gigabit Connection," Scientific American, Oct. 1990, 118 and 120, and Michael L. Dertouzos, "Building the Information Marketplace," Technology Review, Jan. 1991, 28–40.

60. For an alternative analysis, see George Bugliarello, "Toward Hyperintelligence," Knowledge: Creation, Diffusion, Utilization 10 (1988): 67–89.

61. Ibid., 73–78.

62. Ibid., 81–83.

63. Ronald L. Enfield, "The Limits of Software Reliability," Technology Review, Apr. 1987, 36–43, and Michael Rogers, "Can We Trust Our Software?" Newsweek, 29 Jan. 1990, 70–73.

64. Zuboff, In the Age of the Smart Machine, 315–61.

65. René Descartes, Discourse on Method, trans. Laurence J. Lafleur (Indianapolis: Bobbs-Merrill, 1950), 40.

66. Robinson, "Changes in Time Use," 299–300.

67. Brand, The Media Lab, 256.

68. See Simon Blackburn's review of electronic versions of texts by Hobbes, Locke, and Berkeley in Mind 99 (1990): 489–90.

69. Judith Axler Turner, "Museum Computerization: The Evolution Has Begun," Museum News 66 (July–Aug. 1988): 24–25; William H. Honan, "The Museum of the Future: It's All in the Chips," New York Times, 27 Nov. 1988,

sec. 2, 1; and Chris Raymond, "Humanities Researchers Experience a 'Sea Change' in the Use of Computers in Their Disciplines," *Chronicle of Higher Education*, 12 July 1989, A6.

70. Hubert Dreyfus and Stuart Dreyfus, *Mind Over Machine: The Power of Human Intuition and Expertise in the Era of the Computer* (New York: Free Press, 1986).

71. Thomas Aquinas, *Summa Theologica*, pt. 1, quest. 79, art. 3. The active intelligence or intellect is the power with which the soul makes everything. There is also the passive intellect that allows the soul, in a certain way, to become everything.

Chapter Five

1. Aristotle *Nicomachean Ethics* 1139a26–b9; Aristotle *Metaphysics* 1025b18–26, 1064a10–18; and Immanuel Kant, *Critique of Practical Reason*, trans. Lewis White Beck (Indianapolis: Bobbs-Merrill, 1956). Although there is no central and sustained concern with material culture in Western philosophy, occasional discussions of technology and artifacts have been carried on in lively asides and illuminating parentheses. See Carl Mitcham, "Three Ways of Being-With Technology," in *From Artifact to Habitat: Studies in the Critical Engagement of Technology*, ed. Gayle L. Ormiston (Bethlehem, Pa.: Lehigh University Press, 1990), 31–59.

2. Important exceptions are Larry Haworth, *The Good City* (Bloomington: Indiana University Press, 1963), 14–15, 25–38, and Langdon Winner, "Do Artifacts Have Politics?" *The Whale and the Reactor: A Search for Limits in an Age of High Technology* (Chicago: University of Chicago Press, 1986), 19–39. The task, more precisely, is to show how the reality of the material setting is morally charged. To take the material setting merely as an expression of power relations, as the Marxist does, or as a system of information distribution, as Mary Douglas and Baron Isherwood do, is to miss the reality. See Douglas and Isherwood, *The World of Goods* (New York: Basic Books, 1979).

3. I am analyzing moral decisions by asking whether they are daily or fundamental, practical or material, individual or collective. Arrayed in a three-dimensional matrix, these three pairs of distinctions yield eight possibilities. Rather than tediously considering each possibility in turn, I proceed informally to the kind of decision that finally concerns me, to decisions that are fundamental, material, and collective.

4. Gary Larsen, *Beyond the Far Side* (Kansas City, Mo.: Andrews, McMeel & Parker, 1983), [14].

5. Lawrence M. Friedman, *Total Justice* (New York: Russell Sage Foundation, 1985), 55–58.

6. Jane Jacobs, *The Death and Life of Great American Cities* (New York: Vintage, 1961), 3–25.

7. U.S. Bureau of the Census, *Statistical Abstract of the United States 1989* (Washington, D.C.: U.S. Government Printing Office, 1989), 591.

8. Jacobs, *The Death and Life of Great American Cities*, 3–25, and Helen Leavitt, *Superhighway—Superhoax* (New York: Doubleday, 1970), 27, 34, 50, 187–88, 269.

9. A more concerted effort was the establishment of the Office of Technology Assessment by Congress in 1972. While the office's reports are valued for their technical quality and utility, they lack moral judgment and weight. For

background, see Thomas J. Knight, *Technology's Future* (Malabar, Fla.: Krieger, 1982).

10. Robert Reich, "Behold: We Have an Industrial Policy," *New York Times*, 22 May 1988, sec. 4, 29. See also Michael Borrus, "Chips of State," *Issues in Science and Technology* 7 (Fall 1990): 40–48.

11. A more technical and detailed account can be found in my "Texts and Things," in *Lifeworld and Technology*, ed. Timothy Casey and Lester Embree (Washington D.C.: University Press of America, 1990), 93–116.

12. For an illustration of how the scale can slide from the very large to the very small, see Philip and Phylis Morrison, *Powers of Ten: A Book about the Relative Size of Things in the Universe and the Effect of Adding Another Zero* (New York: Scientific American Library, 1982).

13. James E. Larcombe, "Canoe Maker Realizes a Dream," *Missoulian*, 9 Mar. 1986, B3, and C. P. Crow, "The Only Way," *New Yorker*, 22 June 1987, 34–44.

14. Benjamin DeMott, "Hanging Out with Horses," *New York Times Magazine*, 17 Feb. 1985, 65.

15. Norman Maclean, "The Woods, Books, and Truant Officers," in *Norman Maclean*, ed. Ron McFarland and Hugh Nichols (Lewiston, Idaho: Confluence Press, 1988), 81.

16. Lewis Mumford, at the time, was hopeful that the Depression would constitute a crisis more profound and salutary than that. See his *Technics and Civilization* (New York: Harcourt, Brace & World, [1934] 1963), 364–435.

17. Alvin Weinberg, "Can Technology Replace Social Engineering?" in *Technology and the Future*, 5th ed., ed. Albert H. Teich (New York: St. Martin's Press, 1990), 29–38. Though Weinberg conceived of the technological fix, he never thought of it as more than a partial solution to social problems.

18. Daniel Callahan has made a significant start on this problem in *Setting Limits: Medical Goals in an Aging Society* (New York: Simon and Schuster, 1987), and *What Kind of Life: The Limits of Medical Progress* (New York: Simon and Schuster, 1990).

19. Mihaly Csikszentmihalyi, *Flow: The Psychology of Optimal Experience* (New York: Harper & Row, 1990).

20. Crow, "The Only Way," 41.

21. See my "Technology and the Crisis of Liberalism," in *Technological Transformation: Contextual and Conceptual Implications*, ed. Edmund F. Byrne and Joseph C. Pitt (Dordrecht: Kluwer Academic, 1989), 105–22.

22. See my "Republican Virtue in a Technological Society," in *Technological Change and the Transformation of America*, ed. Steven E. Goldberg and Charles R. Strain (Carbondale: Southern Illinois University Press, 1987), 159–75.

23. Haworth, *The Good City*, 145.

24. Michael Walzer has stressed that his argument, in *Spheres of Justice: A Defense of Pluralism and Equality* (New York: Basic Books, 1983), "is radically particularist" (xiv). See also Stephen Toulmin, *Cosmopolis: The Hidden Agenda of Modernity* (New York: Free Press, 1990), 31–33, 188–89.

25. Bernard J. Frieden and Lynne B. Sagalyn, *Downtown, Inc.: How America Rebuilds Cities* (Cambridge, Mass.: MIT Press, 1989).

26. Ibid., 199–213.

27. Lenora Koelbel, *Missoula the Way It Was* (Missoula, Mont.: Gateway,

1972), 29–33.

28. William H. Whyte, *City* (New York: Doubleday, 1988).

29. It was a mental as well as physical straitjacket. See Thomas Michael Power, *The Economic Pursuit of Quality* (Armonk, N.Y.: M. E. Sharpe, 1988), 106–68.

30. Jacobs, *The Death and Life of Great American Cities*, 50–54, and Whyte, *City*, 79–102.

31. Charles E. Little, *Greenways for America* (Baltimore: Johns Hopkins University Press, 1990).

32. A plea for orientation in architecture, along with a critique of placeless universalism, can be found in Kenneth Frampton, "Towards a Critical Regionalism," in *The Anti-Aesthetic: Essays on Postmodern Culture*, ed. Hal Foster (Port Townsend, Wash.: Bay Press, 1983), 16–30, and "Place-Form and Cultural Identity," in *Design after Modernism: Beyond the Object*, ed. John Thackara (New York: Thames and Hudson, 1988), 51–66.

33. See "Public Space," *Dissent* (Fall 1986): 470–85, with contributions by Michael Walzer, Michael Rustin, Gus Tyler, and Marshall Berman; and "Whatever Became of the Public Square?" *Harper's*, July 1990, 49–60, with contributions by Jack Hitt, Ronald Lee Fleming, Elizabeth Plater-Zyberk, Richard Sennett, James Wines, and Elyn Zimmerman.

34. See, for example, Berman, in "Public Space," 478, 480, 483–84.

35. See my "Communities of Celebration," *Research in Philosophy and Technology* 10 (1990): 315–45.

36. Roger Angell, "The Pits and the Pendulum," *New Yorker*, 21 May 1990, 79–83.

37. Frieden and Sagalyn, *Downtown, Inc.*, 252–55.

38. Paul Goldberger considered Battery Park City promising in "Beyond Utopia: Settling for a New Realism," *New York Times*, 25 June 1989, sec. 2, 30.

39. Sennett, in "Whatever Became of the Public Square?" 51.

40. David Cohen and Ben Greenwood, *The Buskers: A History of Street Entertainment* (Newton Abbot: David & Charles, 1981), and Whyte, *City*, 25–55.

41. Christopher Lasch, "The Communitarian Critique of Liberalism," *Soundings* 69 (1986): 60–76.

42. On the balance between guidance and openness in the pursuit of the good city, see Haworth, *The Good City*, 132–41.

43. Brian Barry, review of Michael Sandel, *Liberalism and the Limits of Justice*, in *Ethics* 94 (1984): 525, and Michael Kinsky, in "On Civic Liberalism: A Symposium," *New Republic*, 18 June 1990, 26.

44. Haworth, *The Good City*, 16–17.

45. Ibid., 64–65, 67–69, 119–21; Walzer, *Spheres of Justice*, 3–63; and Berman, in "Public Space," 480–83.

46. John Rawls, *A Theory of Justice* (Cambridge, Mass.: Harvard University Press, 1971), 282–84.

47. For a more general proposal along these lines, see Mickey Kaus, "For a New Equality," *New Republic*, 7 May 1990, 18–27.

48. Hannah Arendt, *The Human Condition* (Chicago: University of Chicago Press, 1958), 38–49, and Sennett, *The Fall of Public Man: The Forces Eroding Public Life and Burdening the Psyche with Roles It Cannot Perform* (New York: Vintage, 1978), 257–340.

49. See for example, Martin Buber, *Eclipse of God: Studies in the Relation between Religion and Philosophy*, trans. Maurice S. Friedman et al. (New York: Harper and Row, 1952); Jacques Maritain, *Approaches to God*, trans. Peter O'Reilly (New York and London: Macmillan, 1954); and Paul Tillich, *Dynamics of Faith* (New York: Harper and Row, 1957).

50. William A. Galston, "Public Morality and Religion in the Liberal State," *Political Science* 19 (1986): 807–24, and Kenneth D. Wald, *Religion and Politics in the United States* (New York: St. Martin's Press, 1987), 1–21.

51. Walter B. Mead, "How Strict Was 'Separation' of Church and State?" *Cross Currents* 26 (1986): 244–47, and Wald, *Religion and Politics*, 102–41.

52. I have it from Carl Mitcham that similar renewals have taken place at the Roman Catholic Cathedral of St. James in Brooklyn and St. Charles Luwanga in Louisville.

53. Kenneth L. Woodward, "The Awakening of a Cathedral," *Newsweek*, 16 June 1986, 59–60, and Ari L. Goldman, "More than a Cathedral: St. John the Divine," *New York Times Magazine*, 15 Nov. 1987, sec. 2, 22–25, 74–76.

54. Goldberger, "Two Gestures of Faith in Religious Landmarks of a Community," *New York Times*, 28 Sept. 1986, sec. 2, 31 and 35.

55. Paul Moore, Jr., "His Final Charge," *Cathedral*, Sept. 1989, 7.

INDEX

Conservatism: disavows responsibility for material culture, 114, 138–39; restrained in shaping society, 3

Consumer vs. citizen, 115–16, 140–41

Control: electronic, over work, 101; modern inclination toward, 2–3. *See also* Power, regardless

Cooperation, informed, 75–77

Copernicus, Nicolaus, 21–22

Corporation: as reflection of Cartesian order, 35–37; decline of, 61; and flexible specialization, 74; and informed cooperation, 77; multinational, in postmodern economy, 63–64; as response to openness of New World, 36

Crafts, as focal reality, 120–21

Csikszentmihalyi, Mihaly, 155n.86, 160n.23, 164n.19

Dante, 101–2

Death penalty, advocacy of, out of resentment, 8

Decision: collective vs. individual, 112–16; fundamental vs. daily, 111; material vs. practical, 111–12

Descartes, René, 22, 24, 35–36, 50, 52

Di Salvatore, Bryan, 152n.19

Discourse: modern, 2–3; postmodern, 3–4, 129, 144. *See also* Narrative; Schema

Disney World, as final hyperreality, 93–94

Divinity: and art, 145–46; in celebration, 135–36

Domestic nature, as focal reality, 120

Donne, John, 22

Dowd, Maureen, 92

Drugs, war on, and resentment, 9–10

Dworkin, Ronald, 19

Eco, Umberto, 83

Economy. *See also* Productivity
—modern: failure of cooperation between industry and government in, 77; decline of rugged individualism in, 64–65; constrained by environment, 62–63; goods saturation in, 63; mass production in, 61, 72; economic totalitarianism as possible successor of, 63–64
—postmodern: defined by information processing, flexible specialization, and informed cooperation, 65; dematerialization in, 60–61; decline of individualism in, 61–62; paradigmatic firm in, 77; resistance to, 77; and economic totalitarianism, 63–64. *See also* Computer; Flexible specialization; Information; Service industry
—United States: decline of, 12–13; federal budget deficit of, 7; foreign debt of, 7; standard prescription for, 13, 126–27

Emerson, Ralph Waldo, 32–33

Eneas, Chief, 29, 30

Engel, Catharine, 72–73

Engels, Friederich, 97

Enlightenment, as unfinished project, 26, 142

Environment: constrains the modern economy, 62–63; and soft vs. hard solutions, 78–79

Episcopalian Church, 145–47

Equal Opportunity, affirmed, 26

Erdrich, Louise, 55–56

Ethics: failure of, to illuminate hyperreality, 94; failure of, to consider material settings, 110–11; particularist, 54–55; universalist, 52–53

Experience, indifferent vs. oriented, 143–44. *See also* Symmetry of reality and humanity

Fagan, Carol, 72–73

Fallows, James, 151n.36

Farmers' Market, 115, 132

Femininism: as critique of aggressive realism, 51; as critique of universalist ethics, 53–55

Information: and human competence, 66–67; instrumental vs.
final, 66; origin of, 66–67; precious commodity before
computers, 75–76
—computerized: and agriculture,
71; and cooperation, 76–77; instrumental, 67–71; final, 71–72.
See also Hyperreality
Information processing, 66–72
Informed cooperation, 75–77
Interstate highway system: as moral
decision, 114; as project of modernism, 34

Jacobs, Jane, 130–31, 132
Japan, and hyperactivity, 18–19
Japanese management, and
hyperactivity, 17
Jefferies, Boyd L., and the perils of
hyperactivity, 15–16
Jefferson, Thomas, 25–26
Jünger, Ernst, 98
Justice: enmeshed in modernism,
26–27; total, as accommodation
of sullenness, 11–12. *See also*
Conservatism; Enlightenment;
Liberalism

Kant, Immanuel, 52–53, 110
Kaus, Mickey, 165 n.47
Koelbel, Lenora, 153 n.35,
164–65 n.27
Kohlberg, Lawrence, 53–54
Kubey, Robert, 155 n.86, 160 n.23
Kyner, James H., 31, 38–39

Labor. *See* Work; Work force
Lakes, Greg, 158–59 n.63
Landmarks, as guides of inquiry,
4–5
Language. *See* Discourse
Larsen, Gary, 111
Larson, Eric, 60
Leiss, William, 152 n.13
Leisure: hyperactive, 101; as passive
consumption, 43–45; sullen, 101
Liberalism: activist in shaping so-
ciety, 3; disavows responsibility

for material culture, 114, 138; no
longer effective, 52–53, 127, 142;
rejects community, 127; and religion, 144; as an unfinished
project, 52, 142. *See also* Enlightenment; Liberal democracy
Liberal democracy, and technology,
81
Linder, Staffan, 101
Locke, John, 22, 24–25, 37–38, 45
Lovins, Amory, 78
Luther, Martin, 22

Marx, Karl, 97–98
McCammon, Joseph Kay, 29–30
Method. *See* Narrative; Procedure;
Schema; Soft vs. hard solutions
Methodical universalism: and the
corporation, 35–37; and science,
35. *See also* Universalism
Michalos, Alex C., 150 n.27
Michelle, Chief, 29
Middle Ages, and origin of modern-
ism, 21–22
Mies van der Rohe, Ludwig, 60
Milwaukee Road, 34, 133, 138
Missoula: baseball park in, 136; beginning of, 131; damaged by
modernism, 129–30; Farmers'
Market in, 132; and the railroads,
30, 31, 34; redevelopment of, 130;
street life in, 131–33
Mitcham, Carl, 149 n.4, 163 n.1,
166 n.52
Mobilization, as social and economic state, 14–15, 98
Modern, etymology of, 20
Modernism: as conjunction of domination of nature, primacy of
method, and sovereignty of the individual, 25; damage of, to cities,
58–59; distinguished as a project
from modernity as an era, 22,
151–52 n.9; in philosophy, 49–50;
and predictions of its end, 20; as
unfinished project, 26, 52–53;
restlessness of, 97–99
Modernity: discourse of, 2–3; distinguished as era from modernism
as project, 22, 151–52 n.9

as possible successor of modern economy, 63–64

Type A, 98–99

Unemployment, as consequence of collective resentment, 9

Universalism: as ethics, 52–53; instantiated in the corporation, 35–37; and science, 50–51; postmodern critique of, 51–52. *See also* Methodical universalism

Verna, Tony, 88

Videogames, as final hyperreality, 91

Vigor, as response to reality, 125–26. *See also* Patience; Symmetry of reality and humanity

Voting behavior, and sullenness, 7–9

Walzer, Michael, 54–55, 164 n.24

Weber, Max, 153 n.47

Weinberg, Alvin, 164 n.17

Whyte, William, 132

Wilderness, as focal reality, 120

Worden, Frank, 131

Wordsworth, William, 28

Work: discipline in computerized, 70; oppressive, 101; as the road to reward and respect, 45. *See also* Flexible specialization; Hyperactivity

Work force, contingent: as consequence of hyperactivity, 16–18; and flexible specialization, 75

Workstation, as instance of instrumental hyperreality, 85

Writing: and hyperintelligence, 105; and reality, 117

Zuboff Shoshana, 68